FEMINIST IN
THE DARK

BLACK WIDOW

DESPERATELY SEEKING SUSAN

CRIMES OF THE HEART

DESERT BLOOM

ALIENS

ALIEN

Desert Hearts

JUMPIN' JACK FLASH

OUTRAGEOUS FORTUNE

FEMINIST IN THE DARK

REVIEWING THE MOVIES

by KATHI MAIO

The Crossing Press, Freedom, CA 95019

Cover design: Diana Souza
Editor: Andrea Chesman

Printed in the U.S.A.

Movie photographs courtesy of Amy Alter Associates,
Book City Collectables, Cinema Collectors, Columbia
Pictures, Fries Home Video; Lorimar Productions, Orion
Pictures, Tri Star Pictures

Author photograph courtesy Dennis Wade

Library of Congress Cataloging-in-Publication Data
Maio, Kathi, 1951-
    Feminist in the dark : reviewing the movies / Kathi Maio
        p.   cm.
    ISBN 0-89594-323-9 :   ISBN 0-89594-322-0 (pbk) :
       1. Women in motion pictures--United States--Reviews. 2. Motion
pictures--United States--Reviews. 3. Feminist criticism.
I. Title.
PN1995.9.W6M33 1988
791.43 '09'093520--dc19   88-21411
                                                CIP

*For Shane Snowdon,
the best editor and sister/pal
a girl could have.*

Acknowledgments

For all they've taught me and shared with me over the years, I'd like to thank the women of two publications. At *Second Wave*, where I published my first feminist writings, I worked with an incredible group of women who shared their skills and vision with great generosity. My love especially to Jane Tuchscherer and Peggy Kornegger for their friendship and support of my writing all these years.

And at *Sojourner*, where I published most of the reviews included in this volume, I'd like to thank Molly Lovelock and Shane Snowden, my editors. Shane and *Sojourner*'s film editor, Susan Shapiro, convinced me to try my hand at film reviews, and then wouldn't let me go back to book reviews once I'd started. For that, my thanks.

Thanks also to Elaine Goldman Gill, for liking those movie reviews enough to want to collect them in a book.

Finally, on a more personal note, I'd like to express my love and gratitude to my parents, Esther and Frank Maio, and to Dennis Wade, my favorite movie (and life) companion.

Preface

Hollywood movies have treated women badly, and continue to do so. Maybe our best response would be for feminist moviegoers and the feminist film critics to simply turn our backs on films from major American studios. That's one approach. It's not mine. The movies I like best to review are general release pop films, the kind that play at every multi-plex cinematic cow palace from coast to coast. I like to review schlock movies because they're the ones I grew up on and feel most comfortable with. But I also think it's important for us to look at the films the majority of Americans are watching. It is the job of the feminist critic to name the distortions and attacks and, by so doing, reject them. If "general" critics did this for us, the feminist press wouldn't need to bother. We could exclusively cover experimental feminist filmmaking, documentaries, animation, and the like. But since we *do* still go to our neighborhood theaters, and since the general press almost always endorses the viewpoint of the dominant culture (ignoring the sexism, racism, elitism, etc. around us), we *do* need to analyze what's out there "at a theater near you."

Here's an example of the problem. One of the reviews included in this collection is of the British "comedy," *Wish You Were Here.* I reviewed that one at the request of a friend who felt betrayed by the film and by the men who reviewed it in several general publications she read before investing her five dollars in a movie ticket. The reviewers had liked the film, identifying it as a lively tale about a "spunky" heroine. Not one identified that heroine as sexually abused. The reason? They just had not *seen* the abuse.

In a similar case, I was overwhelmed by the wholesale racism in the supposedly benign little teen comedy, *Adven-*

tures in Babysitting, and was shocked that most general movie critics seemed to have not even noticed it. I'm not really throwing stones here. I know from my own experience how easy it is to ignore bigotries and how very hard it is to name them. Looking back on the earlier reviews included here, I recognize that my own criticism was much more tentative when I first started out. In my review of *Wildcats*, for example, I identified the fact that there is racism in the story, but I was *much* easier on the film than it deserved. How much of that was due to the charms of Goldie Hawn and the low-keyed feminist content of the film (neither of which *Adventures in Babysitting* can claim) and how much is due to the reluctance of a rookie reviewer to be too unpleasant about a lightweight comedy is hard to say. Since I learned the same bigotries in the same ways (including from movies and television) as the folks who made *Wildcats*, much of what is racist in that film just plain got by me then.

I'd like to think I'd see more today. My voice has, I think, strengthened and my style has become more confident and relaxed over the three years I've been writing movie reviews. At first I was a feminist writer who did film reviews. I think what I've become is a feminist film *critic*, a woman who continues to develop an ever more critical eye toward films. If I have grown stronger, it is in large part due to where I was publishing. In the feminist press I was literally given the space in which to grow. And many women, editors and readers, have helped me get this far by giving me their support and their criticism.

Having an on-going relationship with the feminist press has been a deeply rewarding experience. Not financially, of course. (At least, not before this book—please Goddess!) *Sojourner*, like most feminist, literary, and political publications, cannot afford to pay its writers. But it is hard to put a monetary value on the publishing freedom I've been given at *Sojourner* over the years. When I publish writings for money in various "general" magazines, my words and thoughts have too often been altered by my editors. Then there's the self-censoring I've done, committing to paper only what I thought the editor wanted to see. That's the scariest censorship, and the most difficult to combat.

To have real freedom of expression is worth a great deal. But we all have to make a living, too. Working full-time at another job (in my case, as a librarian) and writing only in our "spare" time doesn't make it any easier. The emotional issues of not getting paid for our writing also require examination. In this lovely capitalist country of ours, it's hard to value your work when it is unpaid. Like many women who publish primarily in unpaid feminist "markets," I find it difficult to even identify myself as "a writer"—and believe it. It is important that the feminist media continue to search for ways to pay women for their writing. To that end, I would urge anyone reading these words to support, in whatever way you can, the feminist newspaper or magazine of your choice. It all depends on you. End of sermon.

A final word about what this book isn't, and what it is. It is not a volume of feminist film theory in the academic sense. If you are looking for analysis of contemporary cinema using psychoanalytic theory or semiotics, you are looking in the wrong place. I have never knowingly used a term like *mise en scene* (although from time to time I have broken down and used the word genre). I mean no disrespect toward the many feminist scholars who have produced an impressive body of scholarship since the early 70s. They are doing valuable work. But film scholars are essentially writing for other film scholars. And I am no film scholar. I'm a film consumer writing for other film consumers.

This collection of reviews is meant to help women (and men with an interest in women's issues) to see women more clearly when they go to the movies. I make no claims, however, that I am presenting the One, True Feminist approach to a particular film. (If Hollywood is no monolith, it's a sure bet feminism isn't!) These are very personal responses to what pleased me in a certain movie, and what ticked me off. Other folks may respond differently. And have.

When I reviewed *Witches of Eastwick*, I embraced it (with reservations) as a woman-affirming subversion of the intense hatred of women expressed by John Updike in his novel of the same name. I later heard from several women who were angered by what they saw as a debasement of their religion, matriarchal wicce ("witchcraft") in this film. They were completely outraged, and right to be so. Yet, at the same time, since I had perceived the three title witches as likable characters, and not as an attack on witches or on women in general, I felt comfortable with what I had written in my review.

Some of the women outraged by *Witches* never saw the film. And that, too, is a valid reaction. We should withhold our money, time, and attention from popular culture that is damaging to us. That's why some feminists have completely sworn off Hollywood films. I can't imagine a day when I'd be one of them.

Let me say it again, I love movies—general audience, schlock flicks—and I always live in hope that when I go to the movies, I'm going to have a good time. Usually I am less than happy as I leave the theater, but sometimes I am very positively surprised. Contemporary horror films, with their vicious and deadly attacks on young women, are some of the most damaging movies currently being produced. Yet when I went to see the film *The Stepfather*, I discovered a psychological horror film with positive, strong images of women. That kind of discovery always feels good.

I'm not willing to give up on movies yet. At the end of a long day we often need those two hours of escape. Feminists can still enjoy American popular films, we need only to work toward being more informed and critical consumers. This collection is a chronicle of my own journey toward being a more critical viewer of the movies I so love. I hope you enjoy it, and that you find it useful in your own exploration of the current movie scene.

Contents

FEMINIST IN THE DARK

Introduction

I can almost hear Joe Chauvinist now. *"Feminist in the Dark?* I'll say! All them libbers are in the dark!"

And, for once, the dear fellow is right. We *are* in the dark, we feminists, when we look at American popular culture, especially Hollywood movies. Like everyone else, we sit in the dark to watch a film. But unlike those who accept current cultural definitions of who women are, feminists are in the dark in another, less comfortable sense. We do not recognize ourselves in what we see. Those women aren't us. They aren't who we want to be either. In fact, the gap between the way women are portrayed on the screen and the way we know ourselves to be is so great (and seems to ever widen) that watching an evening's entertainment invariably leaves us feeling perplexed, bewildered, and more often than not, plain angry.

Moving pictures, one of the great escapist diversions, too often bring women face to face with such sexist realities as violence and exploitation. There's not much escape in that, except in the sense that it makes you feel like running away from the theater!

As Molly Haskell (in *From Reverence to Rape*, 1974) and other critics have observed, the depiction of women by Hollywood actually worsened during the years following World War II and throughout the 60s and early 70s. Three years after Haskell's book (although only haltingly before 1977), Hollywood finally felt, and began to register, the impact of the women's movement. At first, the impact looked like a postive one.

The year 1977 gave us such movies as *The Turning Point* and *Julia*, which showed women questioning their choices, reaching out to one another, and trying to act upon

1

their world. Many other, more problematic films, such as *Looking for Mr. Goodbar*, *Three Women*, and *Annie Hall* also appeared that year. Attack them or defend them, at least they portrayed women as important characters with complex personalities and needs. Joan Micklin Silver's *Between the Lines* (the story, about the staff of a counter-culture newspaper, featured an excellent ensemble cast and gave as much weight to the lives of the women as to the men) was 1977's good omen for non-Hollywood, woman-directed feature filmmaking. In the foreign woman-directed market, Agnes Varda's *One Sings and the Other Doesn't* was a fascinating study of the changes in women's lives during the 60s and 70s.

The year 1978 continued what looked like a hopeful trend of woman-centered movies approaching a feminist viewpoint. Low-budget movies (like Claudia Weill's feature, *Girlfriends*) supplemented the full Hollywood treatment women were now receiving after the long dry spell of the intensely male-focused 60s and early 70s. Consider Paul Mazursky's 1978 neo-woman's picture, *An Unmarried Woman*, staring Jill Clayburgh. It is a much more upbeat variation on earlier unhappy homemaker movies like *Diary of a Mad Housewife* (1970).

Clayburgh's character, Erica, is an upper-middle-class woman who paid her dues as a homemaker (and so insures even a conservative viewer's respect and wishes for happiness), but is dumped by her heartless hubby anyway, which shatters her life. Drawing on her own strength, and the comfort and support of her daughter and woman friends, Erica starts to rebuild her life as a single woman. Of course, her major means of re-establishing her self-esteem is through a new romance with a more enlightened man, but *An Unmarried Woman* is better than most such movies in that regard. Erica is still unmarried at the movie's end. She even decides *not* to go off with Alan Bates, her new (very agreeable) flame. I don't consider Erica the perfect feminist heroine, but compare her to the typical movie heroine of the mid-60s and she looks mighty fine. Regrettably, she looks good in comparison with the majority of women's roles *today*, too.

The most hopeful thing about that 1977-78 season was that many of us viewed it as a sign that the tide had turned. We viewed *Julia* and *An Unmarried Woman* as but the *beginning* of a rich new tradition of women in Hollywood films. We thought movies were only going to get better from that point on. Those of us who fell prey to that level of optimism were, needless to say, proved wrong. The male-dominated culture had not yet begun to fight back.

The 1977-78 season may well represent the high point (since the 30s) of the portrayal of women on film. Since 1978 women have retained many lead roles in films (although not as many leads as the Rambos and Indiana Jones's and Crocodile Dundees of the new macho wave), but it isn't the number of roles that is really in question. It is the way those women's roles are presented that changed, and since those hopeful signs of the 1977-78 season, the changes often have not been for the better. Sexism has, I fear, gotten ever stronger in the movies of the last ten years. Not in the sense of overt, blatant nastiness—although films like *I Spit on Your Grave* (1980) have appeared in sufficient numbers that I am sometimes frightened at the intensity of the vicious cinematic violence against women—but more often in a more subtle, insidious form. It seems that for every sympathetic rendering of the post-feminist woman hero of the late 70s and 80s, there have been three smear jobs.

Not only are the "new" women open to attack, but now that movie chivalry is truly dead and buried, even women playing the "old" roles are open to attack. By the late 70s, you couldn't even count on Mom as a good guy anymore. The maternal role, which, with a few overbearing exceptions, was always aglow with sweetness and light, became fair game for male anger and ridicule. Mother-blaming has become an exceedingly popular Hollywood sport. (They're even laughing at the thought of throwing her from a train!)

3

The ironic thing is that a more realist approach to women's lives as homemakers would have been welcomed by feminists. After all, neither extreme of the mother-whore dichotomy tells our real story, and giving birth doesn't insure one's nomination for sainthood. But realistic images of motherhood aren't what we got.

Look at Meryl Streep's runaway mom in *Kramer vs. Kramer* (1979). Notice how the film manipulates our sympathies toward Dustin Hoffman as the newly sensitized dad and away from the abandoning mother. Even worse is Mary Tyler Moore's suburban mom in *Ordinary People* (1980), directed by everyone's favorite Hollywood liberal, Robert Redford. She's cold, selfish, and destructive. And she must be driven from the house if father (a real sweetheart played by Donald Sutherland) and son are to find love and peace again.

Such movies didn't so much abandon the elements of the idealized mother as transfer them over to the new nurturing daddy figure. In a wicked form of role reversal, moms were increasingly portrayed in ways we associated with the severest type of real-life old-world fathers: as rigid, emotionally cold, harshly judgmental figures.

By 1981 with *Mommie Dearest*, the monster-mother was reaching almost comical proportions. Since that point, you could argue that the backlash has diminished, but I think it has merely changed its form. By the mid-80s, Hollywood no longer felt the need to portray the liberated woman as evil. It became much more effective to promote traditional roles, and then show us as incompetent in filling those roles. The messages of women-oriented movies don't openly attack uppity women so much as chide us into coming to our senses (as if the women's movement was just an adolescent phase we were going through). Gently but firmly, movies now preach that a woman's happiness may include a career, but only when it is combined with a return to an old-fashioned home life.

Diane Keaton in *Baby Boom* (1987) is the perfect example of Hollywood's jolly attack on female independence. Keaton is such an extreme stereotype of the unwomanly career woman that she knows *nothing* of domestic, and especially maternal, matters. (How many women do you know who have no idea how to carry a baby or affix a diaper to its little bottom? I don't know any, either.) Apparently the pursuit of an education and a living are enough to rob a woman of her ability to be a friend, lover, or parent. That is until Motherhood (in this case achieved through the inheritance of an adorable little baby) forces a change.

The bottom line in *Baby Boom* is that women had better return to the good old days, 80s style. Of course, most of us can't afford to quit our jobs and buy a 62-acre spread in Vermont, but the moral still remains: A woman's personal happiness depends upon the joys of motherhood and the love of a good down-home kinda fella. Keaton learns her lesson and finds domestic happiness. A similar, but more brutal lesson is taught to Goldie Hawn in *Overboard*, also released in 1987.

The propaganda geared toward younger women is even more dangerous. In *For Keeps* (1988), Molly Ringwald shows that high school girls can live happily ever after if they only follow their hearts (instead of parental advice to get an abortion or allow an adoption), marry their high school boyfriends, and have their accidental babies. What a great story line for a country already plagued by the tragic consequences of a teen pregnancy epidemic!

Promoting marriage and motherhood is only the first half of Hollywood's one-two anti-feminist punch. The other half is the attack on the unmarried woman, who is shown as unhappy, sexually frustrated, and, at times, mentally imbalanced. Holly Hunter's female lead in *Broadcast News* (1987) doesn't learn the happy lessons accepted by Diane Keaton and Molly Ringwald. And for that reason the audience is invited to believe that she may never be fully happy. Her character, Jane, is married to her career. James L. Brooks (assisted by an absolutely dazzling performance by Ms. Hunter) is smart enough to make Jane a sympathetic character. Since she isn't portrayed, as Keaton was, as a Tiger Lady bitch, it's easier to accept her as a realistic image of a single career woman. But look at her! She's more than sympathetic, she's *pathetic*.

Jane's life is a mess. She can't maintain a relationship. And she is so miserable yet driven that she has to schedule time for her frequent crying jags. She has the same kind of ambition as the two men she works with and is attracted to, but they are able to balance career and relationships. She is not.

At the end of the movie, Albert Brooks is a well-adjusted husband and father, and William Hurt, the bimbo anchor-star, has found just the right gorgeous blonde accessory, whom he is about to marry. Poor Holly doesn't have a man of her own. She *is*, she claims, seeing someone, but we know (from the sexual indecisions and poor interpersonal skills she's demonstrated throughout the film) that she will never be able to find personal happiness until she subordinates her professional ambition to the demands of a traditional love relationship. The fact that Brooks doesn't opt for the romantic solution for his heroine could *almost* be seen as a point in his favor, if he hadn't done such a skillful (not too obvious) job of portraying his female lead as walking basket case.

And if Jane is badly adjusted, think about Alex Forrest in *Fatal Attraction*. It is not by accident that the monster in this psychological thriller is a career woman made mad by her longing for a husband and child. Nor is it surprising that the final shot of that movie (after the monster has been slain) is of Michael Douglas and Anne Archer, reunited husband and wife, walking together into their cozy living room while the camera pans to their family portrait—daddy, mommy, and daughter, all smiling in the idealized (shaken but still intact) nuclear family unit. How eerily similar that shot is to the final shots in Cher's hit movie, *Moonstruck*, in which mother Olympia Dukakis stands by her philandering husband while Cher substitutes one unbearble fiancé for his even crazier younger brother. Disruption of the homestead averted, the happy family toasts "la familia" while the audience views old photos of Italian-American patriarchs and their clans.

There are more real leading roles for women in the movies of the 80s than there were in the 60s and 70s, but now that Hollywood has gotten its act together to present these roles in such a way to criticize the independent woman and praise the traditional woman, it doesn't feel like much of an improvement. Many of the best parts feel like the 40s revisited. Greer Garson and several other actresses of her period made careers out of playing brave mothers. Now contemporary actresses like Jessica Lange and Sally Field are playing those kinds of parts again in films like *Country* (1984) and *Places in the Heart* (1984). Movies of maternal heroism are, in many ways, *good* to see—especially after the mother-bashing of the late 70s and and early 80s. But when films only salute the heroism of women in traditional roles, while questioning the sanity of women who need something more (Meryl Streep in *Plenty*), it taints the positive message of those positive roles.

So things aren't really better than they were ten years ago. In too many cases, they're worse. Erica, our Unmarried Woman, would probably be remarried before the closing credits if that movie were made today. Nevertheless, there are movies made today, even in Hollywood, that portray women in ways we just wouldn't have seen in the 60s. Think of Jane Fonda in that Roger Vadim period she'd love to live down as *Barbarella* (1968), the can't-keep-her-clothes-on astronaut. Now, think about Sigourney Weaver as Ripley in *Alien* (1979) and *Aliens* (1986). Compare Barbarella's sexpot exploitability to Ripley's androgynous beauty and mess-with-me-and-you-die strength. I like to hang onto the fact that the Alien movies were blockbuster hits. Then I try to imagine hit movies like these, with such a female hero, being made and released by a major studio in the late 50s to the late 60s. Hard to imagine, isn't it?

I don't want to project too much gloom. We *have* made progress of sorts at the movies, even if it is through a mine field of anti-feminist backlash. That's why, in collecting these reviews of movies released since 1985, I've tried to balance out my outrage over what's rotten about the ways in which women are still portrayed, with some celebratory joy over recent movies and female roles that were genuinely affirming of women.

In the first chapter, "Joys of Family Life," I start with the nuclear family, but not with overt paeans to family life like *Moonstruck*. The reviews I include here all start with the recognition that the family can be an unhappy, even dangerous place, especially for a young girl. Films like *Desert Bloom* and *Wish You Were Here* can't bring themselves to fully confront issues of family violence and sexual abuse they hint at. They refuse to be completely honest about the damage we do to our young. For that reason, both movies ultimately fail. The documentaries *Streetwise* and *Seventeen* face those issues head on. *Housekeeping* is a lyrical expression of the pain of childhood abandonment and a woman's hunger (no matter what her age) for love, acceptance, and freedom. *The Stepfather* is an ironic send-up of "Father Knows Best" nuclear perfection, disguised as a very effective, very scary psychological horror movie.

Chapter two, "Serious Thoughts About the Lighter Side," looks at the damaging sub-texts of several comedies and one dance movie. *Adventures in Babysitting* and the humor-laced adventure films of Whoopi Goldberg gave me a chance to sound off about Hollywood racism, and *Dirty Dancing* and *Maid to Order* set me to thinking about class issues. Madonna's flop, *Who's That Girl* and Shelley Long's not-so-successful vehicle, *Hello Again*, show why good intentions toward women don't necessarily jive with traditional comedy formulas.

"Women Make Movies" contains reviews of several films directed by women and is just as much a mixed bag of pans and praise as any of the other sections of the book. The emergence of the woman feature film director in the late 70s and 80s is not, in and of itself, the solution to the problem of Hollywood sexism. Women directors, like woman doctors, come out of the same training grounds as the guys and (for the most part) have to fund their projects from the same production system. Joan Freeman, who got her feature start, like so many, in the "exploitation" market, is still showing the ill effects in her latest film, *Satisfaction*. The mother-daughter effort, *The Allnighter*, directed by Tamar Simon Hoffs, and starring her daughter of rock band (The Bangles) fame, is just plain rotten. On the other hand, independents like Donna Deitch and Lizzie Borden, and non-Hollywood filmmakers like Canada's Patricia Rozema and Australia's Gillian Armstrong, are making good films on tiny budgets that say new and exciting things about women in the bargain. What remains to be seen is whether women directors of the 90s will be able to break into Hollywood without breaking faith with other women. I still believe women writing, producing, directing, and acting will make a positive change. We shall see.

The chapter "Women Together and Divided" includes films that show our relationships with one another. There are women brought together by a place or profession (*Steaming*, *Working Girls*), by blood (*Crimes of the Heart*), by friendship (*Witches of Eastwick*), and by animosity over a man (*Outrageous Fortune*). How women get along, or don't, is a source of endless fascination since it is something we have seen so little of in films of the last thirty years. What Hollywood has to show us isn't always a pretty picture, but it is certainly one worth studying.

"Of Lovers and Husbands" is a real mix of movies that show women in relationships with men. *Heartburn* shows us a marriage disintegrating. *Compromising Positions* shows us a troubled marriage that sticks. Peggy Sue looks back on her decision to marry a loser, and Joan Wilder of *Jewel of the Nile* (both played exceptionally well by

9

Kathleen Turner) can't decide whether to stick by her beach-bum lover either. Since this is Hollywood, you can have little doubt what their final decisions will be. Movies of the 80s no longer feel obliged to idealize modern men. And why should they bother, since they always "get the girl" anyway? Hollywood has taken to promoting the "Smart Women, Foolish Choices" school—and seems to endorse it completely.

And last, but assuredly not least, is a section of suspense film reviews under the heading "The Mysteries of the Modern Woman." Mysteries, in both book and movie form, are my first love. The femme fatales of film noir, and good-girl mystery heroines trying to protect themselves in a world of violence provide some of film's most fascinating (although not necessarily most positive) images of women. Women in recent suspense films remain captivating. I've included reviews of films that are good, bad (and I mean horrid), and in-between when it comes to the way they treat women.

Black Widow serves women well. *Fatal Attraction* is an abomination. Both were hit movies. The lure of well-crafted suspense is equally strong in both. Hollywood has always been able to hypnotize us with the most outrageous flights of misogyny. You *might* wonder how any woman could enjoy (perhaps to the point of joining in as the theater audience screams out "Kill her!") the kind of misogyny shown in *Fatal Attraction*, but most folks don't wonder about it at all. To me, the scariest thing about the distortion of women in film is how often we sit in the dark and soak up those images—colors, characters, emotions—and internalize their damaging woman-hating messages, without consciously recognizing them. We can leave the theater with a happy heart, never knowing we've been had. Never fully realizing that we've just been attacked.

I make it sound like some grand conspiracy, don't I? Well, I don't mean to suggest that there is one fiendish, satanic patriarch tucked away in Burbank somewhere, plotting how to do the most possible damage to women each day.

Obviously, that's not the way it is. And I know that I some-times make "Hollywood" sound like an evil monolith. That's not true either. What *is*, I think, true is that the American film industry is a male-dominated, profit-oriented business ruled by two mottoes: Nothing succeeds like Success, and Nothing succeeds like Excess.

Hollywood simply reflects and magnifies the patriarchy that created it. But it has to make it really big to fit the giant screen. Fueled by anti-feminist backlash, and driven by the need to go for more and more shocking and spectacular effects, many filmmakers have treated women worse in the last ten years than at any time in the past. For example, the misogynist violence of Hitchcock's later ("torture the heroine") period has been duplicated and magnified by several generations of male film school graduates. The psycho is now a full-scale slasher, a guy who's never met a woman he didn't want to kill.

While they are still being made (*Friday the 13th, Part 52* should be out any day now), slasher movies may have just about run their course. I wish I could say the same for the ultra-macho school of the Stallones and Schwarzeneggers. The Mr. Universe anti-heroes are as monsyllabic and fero-cious as ever. And they bring in millions at the box office.

Except for the occasional Ripley, who can beat the muscle boys at their game, women aren't packing them in with the same numbers. And yet, today's movies aren't all macho men and chain-saw killers. And it's not all heavy-handed backlash either. More and more of the low-budget, low-promotion movies hitting theaters (and even a few of the big-budget, big-promotion films, like Penny Marshall's appropriately titled *Big*) are directed and/or written by women. Usually nonviolent and women-focused, most such recent releases fall into the category of genial turkeys, movies that will never win any awards for technical brilliance or feminist politics, but which are nonetheless enjoyable and, by and large, unobjectionable in their portrayal of women.

In the last few weeks, I've seen *Casual Sex?*, *Sticky*

Fingers, and *Assault of the Killer Bimbos*. Even the titles are a giveaway that none of them deserve a nomination for Feminist Film of the Year. The best of the three, *Sticky Fingers*, written and produced by Melanie Mayron and Catlin Adams, with Adams directing leads Helen Slater and Mayron, is a warm, funny "fable" about how money can almost ruin a beautiful friendship. Unfortunately, the two buddy leads are total dingbats who, when presented with cold cash, can't control their lust for shopping.

Casual Sex?, directed by Genevieve Robert and written by Wendy Goldman and Judy Toll, wasn't able to completely free itself from the stage conventions of its theatrical beginnings. Worse, it wasn't able to free itself from the conclusion that a husband and kids are what it's all about. Still, it says some good things about women's sexuality (and some sacrilegious things about male sexuality), things that you've *never* heard uttered in movies written and directed by men.

And at the bottom of the pack is the D-movie, *Assault of the Killer Bimbos*, a proud-to-be-rotten drive-in movie directed by Anita Rosenberg. The lead bimbos consist of two go-go dancers and a truck stop waitress. And, yes, they all prance around in halter tops and hotpants. But they can defend themselves and each other from cops and hit men, fix cars (with hair spray and nail polish remover), and still manage to have fun in the sun, so it's not really as bad as it sounds.

Junky as these three movies are, they express a genuine affection for women, and they allow their multiple female leads to show real affection and love for one another. It almost makes me see good omens again. But I'm older and wiser than in '77. I'm controlling my optimism this time around. Besides, how far have we really come when we're only as far as we were when Hollywood made bad-girl comedies and melodramas before the Hays Code clamped down? Recently I saw Jean Harlow in *Redheaded Woman* (1932) for the first time. As written by Anita Loos, Harlow's openly sexual gold digger was hard as nails and bold as brass, but she was loyal to her best woman buddy and lived happily—but not virtuously—ever after. Very nontraditional. A lot of fun.

There's progress for you. On our *good* days, we've come as far as 1932.

The Joys of Family Life

Desert Bloom

Pink-Ribbon Cop-out

I sometimes wonder what it would be like if Hollywood ever made an honest film about realistically portrayed people. They have worked so hard for so long to create and maintain an elaborate mythology about American life that I suspect they are incapable of even approaching reality. Muriel Rukeyser's prediction in her famous poem about Käthe Kollwitz probably applies to the folks out in La La Land who hold the purse-strings of the film industry. If they ever made a film that told the truth about one woman or one family, the world would split open.

That, of course, is why so many of us rely on independently produced "art" films for our more thoughtful entertainment. But even independent filmmakers face their own grim reality—that of a conglomeratized, conservative film industry that must be utilized for *some* financial backing, or at least for decent distribution of the final product. I don't know whether it is this marketplace reality or a general lack of human understanding that made so beautiful a film as *Desert Bloom* into such an ultimately disappointing experience. But, to me, Eugene Corr's first feature film is a clear example of a (pardon my antiquated slang) cop-out.

Desert Bloom is the story of the Chismore family during a two-month period beginning in December 1950. The heavy-handed theme is one of the nuclear family (represented by the Chismores) coming to crisis at the dawning of the nuclear age (represented by the first A-bomb test at the Nevada Gunnery Range on January 27, 1951). Despite the studied profundity of the movie's premise, the first half of *Desert Bloom* is an unqualified success, due, in large part, to the viewpoint of the film: that of thirteen-year-old Rose Chismore.

You will hear from various sources that *Desert Bloom* is a Jon Voight film. Don't you believe it. This film is firmly in the possession of an incredibly gifted young actress (a thirteen-year-old schoolgirl from Cedar Falls, Iowa) named Annabeth Gish. Gish, as Rose, is the central figure in this film, and she, at least, is absolutely true.

Rose lives in a small house next to a trailer camp in that strange zone on the outskirts of Las Vegas where neon glitz surrenders to the vast desert. Rose's real father abandoned her mother, two little sisters, and Rose herself when she was six. The current family patriarch and self-proclaimed protector is an alcoholic WWII veteran, Jack Chismore (Jon Voight), who married Rose's mother Lily (Jobeth

Rose Chismore (Annabeth Gish, left) receives support and kinship from her Aunt Starr (Ellen Barkin) in Desert Bloom.

Williams) when Rose was nine. We are told that, after the wedding, Rose attempted to protect her mother by clobbering Jack with a frying pan. The relationship has continued to be a troubled one.

Rose is now coming of age in a home where fear, frustration, and resentment are rife. The tension is almost palpable. Her mother copes by doggedly clinging to a Norman Rockwell image of her family. She is a manic cheerleader, leading the children in sing-alongs and spouting a homey maxim for every unhappy occasion. When things get too bad she has a relapse of compulsive gambling. But mostly she struggles to be the perfect working mother of the 50s. She gets no help from "Daddy" with housework or shopping. Meals are what's quickest, like a revolting goulash of Campbell's mushroom soup and tuna fish over Minute rice.

Stepfather Jack operates a last chance gas station on the edge of the desert. His injuries from the war go beyond a bad leg. He is plagued by flashbacks and hides liquor bottles throughout the house to help him push back the memories and his feelings of inadequacy. He is abusive when drunk and his favorite target is, not suprisingly, Rose. Rose, who has not yet acquired her mother's skill at self-delusion and selective vision, sees through all Jack's weakness and hypocrisy and, in so doing, threatens his tenuous hold on male authority.

The relationship between Jack and Rose, which is the key relationship in the film, seems an almost textbook case study of incest. Yet Eugene Corr, who wrote as well as directed the film, totally skirts this issue. For the comfort level of the audience, this was a wise decision. For the honesty of the film, I am not so sure. There *is* a great deal of honesty in the complexity of the relationship. Jack is proud of his bright, brave stepdaughter. He desperately wants to see unquestioning love shining from Rose's eyes, as it does from the two younger girls'. When he can't have that, he sometimes settles for a look of fear and humiliation. At the same time, Rose's resentment of her stepfather is equaled only by her desperate need for his male approval. When Jack is hospitalized after one particularly bad binge, Rose tells us in voice-over, "I was happy he was gone, and afraid he wouldn't come back." A haunting summary of life in the patriarchy.

Enter Aunt Starr (Ellen Barkin). Like the atom bomb in the desert (another bit of heavy-handed symbolism here!), Starr brings a new, explosive element into the Chismore home. She is the glamorous aunt who, in violation of all the clampdown rules of the 50s, seems totally in touch with her sexuality. Revels in it, in fact. She visits her sister's family long enough to establish the forty-two days' residence needed for a quickie divorce. She represents self-confidence and sophistication to young Rose. More important, she is the ally and mentor Rose so desperately needs.

The first half of *Desert Bloom* is really an exquisite film. In a collage of many small scenes, Corr sets up the various relationships and the upcoming crisis. We are also given an often humorous, almost nostalgic look at the early 50s. America's unquestioning love affair with technology is everywhere. The Hoover Dam is an exciting family outing. Las Vegas schoolchildren are typed for blood, issued dog tags, and drilled constantly in the ways to stay safe during a nuclear attack (hide your head and don't look at the white flash). Yet the horror and absurdity of these precautions is lost on the people of Nevada in their pride in being the home of this new technology. Daddy renames his station "Jack's Atomic Gas" and young women vie for the title of "Miss A-Bomb."

Desert Bloom finally fails because of Corr's inability or unwillingness to *honestly* follow through with the situations he has created. The family crisis is precipitated by Rose's discovery of Starr and Jack in a drunken embrace, an embrace that Starr incites. But what is Starr's motivation for a sexual come-on to Jack? Is it that she has been exploited and abandoned by a new lover? A strange and, to me, unbelievable motivation. Or are we to believe, as the people of 1950 would undoubtedly have believed, that looks are not deceiving—that a woman who dresses like a bimbo is, indeed, a bimbo? If Corr believes that, he forgot to tell Ellen Barkin. Barkin plays the role in defiance of any stereotype. Starr's idea of fashion may be straight out of Frederick's of Hollywood, and she may strive for validation through the sexual attraction of men, but she also has some self-respect. And she loves Rose. Would she actually come on to the man who had quite recently, and with no justification, brutalized a beloved niece? I don't think so.

It is at this point that the film falls apart. Major familial conflict ensues, in a scene that is at times funny but never believable. Then, just before the dawn's early light, with that first mushroom cloud on the horizon, a tentative reconciliation takes place in the Chismore home. The adult voice of Rose informs us that although it was never easy for Jack, "the worst times were over."

It is the kind of pink-ribbon ending that Hollywood loves, but it is an outrage to the sensitivity and honesty of the first half of the film. Jack Chismore is not a monster, but he is a deeply troubled man. There is no princess kiss or fairy godmother, or even a veterans' group therapy organizaton to transform him into a healthy, loving man. The next time he gets drunk, he will humiliate or beat (or possibly rape) Rose. And what would it do to Rose—sensitive, intelligent Rose—to spend five more years in that kind of environment? One shudders to think. And because even filmmakers sponsored by the "socially conscious" Sundance Institute (of Robert Redford) hate to leave an audience shuddering, Eugene Corr lies to us instead.

The main reason Corr's cop-out as screenwriter infuriates me is that it is so unfair to the actors in *Desert Bloom*. There isn't a false performance in the movie, and, considering the material they had to work with, that is a remarkable accomplishment. Voight gets at the vulnerability as well as the violence of Jack. Jobeth Williams makes us believe that there is someone living behind Lily's frenzied sunniness, and Ellen Barkin is fabulous. As for Annabeth Gish, she makes this deeply flawed film a must-see. She makes the intensity of being thirteen years old so real that it resonates in our memory, bringing back the pain and excitement we all felt.

She also makes me believe that, in spite of all the damage Jack did and would probably continue to do, Rose Chismore would be a survivor. No pink ribbon. That's a happy ending, too.

The Stepfather

Daughter Knows Best

I have never been a big fan of horror movies. And, as for what passes for horror movies these days...Well, the biggest horror is that people make these things—and that other people go to see them. It's been a steady downhill ride since Hitchcock made his brilliant and misogynist ground breaker of modern horror in *Psycho* (1960).

The knife- (ax-, drill-, power saw-) wielding psychopath has completely displaced the more innocent Misunderstood Monster as horror hero. Now *they* really were heroic, those large, awkward, ugly creatures who only wanted to be loved and free. *Tragic* heroes, of course. They repelled the very people they wanted to reach out to. And the general populace wanted to hunt them down, to kill or imprison them for being unruly—and different. Such movies could touch the feelings of insecurity and "otherness" in all of us. King Kong, Frankenstein, even Godzilla were the kind of monsters I could relate to, even root for.

Not so, *Psycho*'s Norman Bates! Norman nonetheless became a real trend-setter. During the 60s and early 70s, the psychopath shared the screen with a few other short-lived horror fads. There were the Deranged Old Lady movies (*What Ever Happened to Baby Jane*, 1962; etc.). Then the Children of Hell films (*Rosemary's Baby*, 1968; *The Exorcist*, 1973; etc.) spit fire at us for a while. You could write books on just these two types of horror movies, and what they seemed to be saying about the minds, bodies, and spiritual integrity of women of all age groups. Talk about damned-if-you-do/damned-if-you-don't! These horror films seemed to suggest that if you didn't marry, you'd become grotesquely warped, and if you did, you'd probably get knocked up by Satan and carry a cursed fetus. And if it wasn't cursed to begin with, your kid (especially if you're a single mother) would soon become the property of the devil.

These formulas were popular for a time, and each is revived for a picture or two every once in a while. But their success pales in comparison to the crimson glory of the horror formula, closely tied to *Psycho*, that took hold of the marketplace in 1978. It has been given many titles: Slasher, Dead Teenager, Knife Kill, Slice-n-Dice, Splatter, Cut-n-Slash, and Gusher, to name a few. Take your pick. They're all quite descriptive of the type of horror film that has remained box-office (and home video) champ since John Carpenter released his original *Halloween* ten years ago.

There is some variation from film to film, but the basic formula consists of a psychotic (almost always male) going on a rampage through suburban homes, high schools, or other salubrious settings. Our psycho prefers messy weapons that will produce the most bloodshed when he slaughters the local citizenry (usually young, usually female).

Not only is the typical victim a teenaged woman, she is generally also pretty and quite shapely, *and* at the point of her sexual discovery. Scenes of her alone in her room or petting with a boyfriend usually afford the audience with several glimpses of breasts or female buttocks before she is slaughtered. The frightening message of these films seems to be that girls who are sexual, girls who don't keep their bodies covered at all times (even in the privacy of their homes), are asking for it. "It" being a form of sexual release (for the psychotic killer) that can be achieved only by use of a knife or chain saw or power drill as he rips apart young female flesh and snuffs out all life within it.

If I hadn't seen these films with my own eyes, I don't think I'd believe that they exist. Just think about the use of the psychopathic murderer as a horror hero. King Kong was a monster we were supposed to root for. Are we supposed to cheer for a madman who rips apart young women? Judging from audience reaction in darkened movie theaters, I fear the answer is yes.

How can men hate and fear us so much that they need to play out these kinds of fantasies? If it were only a few sicko filmmakers who sold these movies from under the counter of some sleazy storefront to men in desperate need of professional help, it wouldn't be so scary. But *millions* of people see these films, making producers (some of whom, like Debra Hill of the *Halloween* series, are women) very rich. Women filmmakers even write and direct these movies.

Amy Jones and Rita Mae Brown teamed up to create *The Slumber Party Massacre*, which is just as bad as anything men have made. Of the eleven—count them, eleven—victims offed by a man and his power tool, more than half are female. Jones makes sure to give us a shower room scene (with camera close-ups of several soapy female posteriors) and more than one clothes-changing scene with bare-breasted posing. The killer actually says to one of his victims, "You want it. You love it," as he brings his drill down on her! The film isn't scary so much as sickening.

What *could* these women have been thinking of? Money, one can only assume. They would probably claim that they were trying to spoof the slasher genre, but I wouldn't buy that story with a wooden nickel. They objectify women as sexual objects and then kill them. That's no way to make a living. (A second *Slumber Party Massacre* has just been released, also from a woman filmmaker, Deborah Brock. I haven't had the stomach to watch it.)

Now that I've convinced you that horror films are the most vicious form of misogynist fantasy around today, that such films, even in the hands of women, are loathsome and disgusting and devoid of redeeming social value, let me throw you a curve. Horror films can provide positive images of women as good, attractive, sexual people who can prevail in the face of male violence. With a minimum of gushing gore and flashy violence, a horror film can be truly frightening. It can have your heart racing. It can raise a gasp or a scream and still make you feel like there's hope for the human race when you leave the theater. Best of all, it's possible for such a film to be made by men. I know it's possible, because I've just seen it.

The film is *The Stepfather*. It was directed by Joseph Ruben and written for the screen by Donald E. Westlake. It is a story that feels real because it was based in fact. Westlake read a news story about a New Jersey man who killed his entire family. He changed his name and career, and then started a new life with a new marriage. With Carol Lefcourt and Brian Garfield, Westlake devised a nightmarish scenario. What if you were such a man's next family?

The Stepfather wastes no time in setting up the horror of the situation. As the camera pans from a quiet suburban street into the second floor of a handsome home, we see a bearded man (Terry O'Quinn), spattered with blood, methodically clean up. He showers, cuts and shaves off the beard, puts on contact lenses, and dons a dapper, professional suit, complete with argyle sweater-vest. When he's ready to face the world, he enters the hallway, spots a toy sailboat and puts it away in a toy box in the nearby bedroom. As he goes down the stairs, we see blood on the wall. And, as he stops to straighten up a few more things, we spy a woman's body in the background and a child's body in the foreground. He exits the house, whistles a merry "Camptown Races," picks up the paper from the lawn, and strolls away down the street.

In the next scene, a year later, he is named Jerry Blake and is married to a lovely widow with a teenaged daughter. To Susan (Shelley Hack), Jerry is a second chance at happiness. To daughter Stephanie (Jill Schoelen), he is a father-figure she wants no part of. He *seems* nice enough. He even buys her a puppy. But when he touches her, she can't help but recoil. And when her repeated troubles at school lead to an expulsion, she sees the flash of something in his eye, "like he wanted to erase me off the face of the earth," she tells her best friend.

Everyone puts Steph's bad attitude at home and school down to her inability to accept her real father's death, but the audience knows better. We know that what Stephanie senses, but is unable to articulate, is real danger. But to the rest of this suburban Seattle community, Jerry is the All-American family man. He sells real estate for American Eagle Realty. He watches "Mr. Ed" re-runs before retiring and making love to his wife. He's a concerned step-parent who'll plead for a second chance for his recalcitrant new daughter. He putters in a workshop in the basement, building birdhouses.

The sickness is there in everything, only no one sees it—but Stephanie and the audience. This is a man for whom the happy American nuclear family is a religious icon. But Jerry's Norman Rockwell perfection isn't real. Stephanie recognizes it as a "fantasy thing" where she and her mother are expected to "be like the families on TV....Grin and laugh and be having fewer cavities all the time."

Because Jerry's fantasies are nothing more than "The American Dream," and his views are those of the All-American patriarch, they seem normal to the adults around him, even when they are clearly crazy. In the most chilling scene of the movie, at a backyard barbecue, Jerry shares a few beers around the picnic table with five other family men. One of them points out the follow-up story in the Seattle paper about the man who wiped out his family a year earlier. What would cause a man to kill his family, they wonder. "Maybe they disappointed him," Jerry suggests. And not one man remonstrates.

At that same barbecue, Stephanie gets a full look at what she has glimpsed before. While retrieving ice cream from the basement freezer, she surprises Jerry "letting off steam." The man has lost it, but his psychotic outburst switches off to a "Hi, Honey," when he spots Stephanie. Jerry knows he has made a tactical error. And Stephanie knows now that she is right, that Jerry is an evil presence in the house of her mother. She resolves to expose him. And the rest of the movie is a psychological duel between the two.

There are other players. Stephanie's psychiatrist, played by Charles Lanyer, respects Stephanie's instincts enough to try to find out what kind of man this stepfather is. And the brother of Jerry's last wife/victim is also on his trail. Stephen Shellen plays the grieving brother like a road warrior vigilante. Between the two men, you feel sure that one of them will gallop up to the Blake household in time to save the women and children.

Think again. But really, I can say no more about the plot. That would ruin it for you. And you really should see this film. Let me only say that it is the most woman-affirming horror film I have ever seen. It is scary and suspenseful and sometimes terrifyingly violent, but in ways that are never exploitive and which never rely on a river of blood. The way *The Stepfather* thumbs its nose at slasher movies in the very last scene, with the female destruction of a phallic/nuclear family symbol, is alone enough to recommend it.

But there is so much more that makes this a great horror film. The sly, satiric humor of Westlake's script is a cut (if you'll excuse the pun) above anything in recent memory. Joseph Ruben's direction matches it perfectly. Ruben never resorts to the obvious or the overblown shock effect. He tells his story quietly but with full use of dramatic tension. The arty touches are there (Hitchcock references include shower and stair shots, a stuffed bird in the Blake dining room, and a flock of its living but uneasy brethren shown perched on a telephone wire during the movie's climax), but they are never intrusive.

And the cleverness of the writing and direction are served well by some sterling performances. Jill Schoelen is wonderful as the teen heroine. And there is no way to describe the performance of Terry O'Quinn as the psychopath who wants nothing more than the perfect nuclear family. For those used to bug-eyed frenzy in such parts, O'Quinn's nondescript normalcy—blink and you'll miss the split-second of rage that breaks through his bland smile from time to time—is absolutely chilling. This is O'Quinn's first starring role. If there is any justice in this world, it won't be his last.

Who would believe that I'd be giving a rave review to a horror film? It shocks even me. But this is a movie that really deserves it, not only for what it is, but for what it represents. Filmmakers occasionally make a social drama or sophisticated comedy that treats women with respect. But when was the last time a *horror* film did? Slasher movies can be made with no-name casts, a zero budget, and, as long as the women whimper and their blood flows freely, they'll pack them in and make big bucks. *The Stepfather*, which respects women and the intelligence of its viewers, violates every standard operational procedure of current horror filmmaking. It will probably be a flop. Respect for women doesn't go over big in this country. How's that for horrifying?

Housekeeping

Coming Home by Leaving It

Even though Bill Forsyth is one of my favorite contemporary filmmakers, I didn't think he could pull off an adaptation of Marilynne Robinson's brilliant first novel (and feminist cult classic), *Housekeeping*. I trusted he could handle the emotions involved. After all, loss, acceptance, loneliness, caring, quirky individuality, and a gentle, absurd sense of humor are all staples of his wonderful films, which include *Gregory's Girl, Local Hero*, and *Comfort and Joy*. Scotland's foremost director could capture the heart and humor of Robinson's characters, I had no doubt, but could he handle their womanity?

For me, Forsyth's own maleness wasn't an issue, but the fact that his heroes and the great majority of his characters have heretofore been male was. Women are usually such sketchy and mysterious creatures in his work. They aren't stereotypes, to be sure. You'd be hard-pressed to find a mindless sex kitten or grasping shrew in the lot. Neither are they powerless.

Maddy, the light-fingered and life-loving woman who packs up and leaves one evening, so laying to waste the life of *Comfort and Joy*'s DJ protagonist "Dickie Bird," is a fascinating character. But she is on the screen for all of about five minutes. The conspiracy of teenaged women in *Gregory's Girl* ("It's just the way girls work. They help one another.") is likewise very appealing. But there is no doubt who the star of the film is. It is Gregory. In *Local Hero*, Marina and Stella are women we want to know. But we never get the chance to. All the screen time is spent with the four male leads. Forsyth's women unquestionably have their own stories to tell. But Bill, always too busy examining the lives of his loser lads, has never taken the time to tell them. Until now.

If women characters were simply support players in Forsyth's earlier work, men are mere supernumeraries in *Housekeeping*. Only one male character, the sheriff, appears in more than one scene. This is, from beginning to end, the story of a family of women within The Family of Women. And it is a story of great beauty.

Ruthie (Sara Walker) and her younger sister Lucille (Andrea Burchill) have been abandoned again and again in their young lives. Their father, they never knew. And their mother, Helen, was a distant, glamorous creature during the few years they shared with her.

Sylvie (Christine Lahti, right) offers a cake to Ruthie (Sara Walker, left) and Lucille (Andrea Burchill) in Housekeeping.

Helen (Margot Pinvidic), who seems always preoccupied with her own dreams and demons, one day takes action against them. She borrows a friend's car, leaves Seattle, and returns to the home of her mother in rural Fingerbone. There she deposits her two small daughters in the front room with a bag of cookies and an admonition to share them. She drives to an open field to eat wild berries and sun herself on the roof of her car, and then, with cheerful determination, drives off a cliff into the same lake that had long ago claimed her father in a spectacular train wreck.

Orphaned, the two girls live and grow under their grandmother's watchful eye until the morning she fails to awaken. Two great-aunts are then called in to take over. Lily (Anne Pitoniak) and Nona (Barbara Reese) are financially enriched by their rent-free accommodations, but the isolation of rural life and the responsibilities of child care are too much for them. When they receive a short note from Helen's long-lost "itinerant" sister, Sylvie, they waste no time in calling her home and beating a fast retreat to Spokane.

Sylvie (Christine Lahti) is a vague, benevolent woman who shows up at the door one day, a single suitcase in hand, wearing newspaper insulation and a shiny dress under a shapeless and tattered raincoat. She accepts the responsibilities of a household and two children with placid goodwill that belies her sacrifice. Sylvie's real home is the road and the rail, not the house of her mother. Still, she willingly settles down to her own rendition of "housekeeping." She fills the house with cans, newspapers, cats, and her gentle gypsy spirit.

For the bashful and awkward Ruthie, Sylvie is kindred both by blood and temperament. Sylvie doesn't praise or scold; she accepts Ruthie with an unstated, unconditional affection that makes fashionable clothing and scrubbed floors unimportant. But Lucille, equally loved, has other needs.

Lucille wants to eat a nutritious dinner in a clean kitchen with the lights on. She wants to be just another teenaged girl concerned about friends, school, and the latest hairdos and fashions. She covets discipline and order. Normalcy. And when she knows, at last, that the comforts of conventionality are the one thing Aunt Sylvie will never be able to give her, Lucille does what she has to do to get them for herself.

Had Mr. Forsyth been a Hollywood director, I fear that he would have succumbed to the temptation to make Lucille the villain of the piece. He does not. How could he? Lucille is *us*: people who think of home as a place, and who never hear (or hope to hear) hidden voices chanting, "It's better to have nothing."

Barring Lucille, he might have made the sheriff and the town's churchwomen the bad guys—harsh, interfering busybodies. He does not. The people of Fingerbone are unassuming and caring folk who worry about a young girl kept out all night by an aunt who sees nothing wrong in hopping a ride home in the boxcar of a freight train.

They have reason to worry. For most of us, Sylvie is both an attractive and repulsive figure. She is a woman belonging to no society but her own. In truth, most of us, like the people of Fingerbone, would hate to see a child we care about in the custody of an unkempt woman who balances on the edge of a bridge in her leisure moments, or who tries to tempt wood sprites out into the open by leaving marshmallows on the twigs of small trees.

What they and we don't know, until Robinson and Forsyth show us, is that this fey, transient woman is exactly the guardian Ruthie needs. Ruthie never finds her home until the moment when Sylvie warms her and embraces her within the folds of her grubby coat, with the lost children of the woods silently singing around them. Ruthie never feels blessed until the moment when, riding in a boxcar with Sylvie and an old woman, Sylvie tells the woman simply, "She's a good girl." Bobbing around in a leaky (and stolen) rowboat, cold and hungry, in the middle of the night, singing "Goodnight, Irene" with Sylvie is just what Ruthie needs to sustain her.

The rest matters little. When the churchwomen come to call and murmur over Ruthie's sad life, Sylvie admits that Ruthie "*is* sad." "Who wouldn't be?" she asks. Yet *Housekeeping* is not a sad story, because there is nothing sad about the way Sylvie and Ruthie find family in one another. That is why, when the two are "cast out to wander," their leave-taking touches them (and us) not as a tragic occurrence, but as an apotheosis: an act of pure joy and release. For Ruthie and Sylvie, if not for Lucille and the rest of us, coming home means leaving "home," the keeping of a house, behind us.

The performances in this lovely movie are intricate and moving. Such might be expected from Christine Lahti, who, as a support player, has consistently outshone the stars she was hired to support. There is nothing sentimentalized about her Sylvie. She is raw, weird, and spellbinding. It is a brave performance not only for its depth, but also for its total lack of leading lady vanity and femininity. To play such a part, in such a way, in your first starring role, is to invite Hollywood to give you nothing but "character" parts for the rest of your career. With Lahti's range and, yes, beauty that would be a real pity.

The performances of Sara Walker and Andrea Burchill are possibly even more impressive than Lahti's, coming as they do from less experienced performers cast as characters even more difficult to depict. Burchill's Lucille is extraordinary in her ordinariness. She is so small and courageous. We can almost see "Ozzie and Harriet" playing behind her eyes, and it's enough to break your heart. And Sara Walker, as Ruthie, faces the greatest challenge of all. She must play a gawky, shy lump of a girl and make us see the magic behind her passive exterior.

The highest praise must, however, go to Bill Forsyth for the faithfulness of his screenplay to the words of Marilynne Robinson and for the tenderness of his direction.

I'd like to call this film "a triumph," but such a designation is far too trite, appearing as it does, undeservedly, on every other movie ad you see. Now that we have a film that finally deserves giant ads and extravagant praise, it's highly doubtful that you'll see any ads at all, with or without the word "triumph" attached.

Housekeeping is one of those films the major studios, in this case Columbia, dump quietly onto the market to quickly disappear. They place it in only a few movie houses (only fourteen in the entire country, if the *Wall Street Journal* is to be believed) in a handful of cities. In the feeble and unimaginative brains of the honchos in the Italian suits, a film of such humanity and gentle humor, a film with so few men and so many women, and a film with no violence, villains, sex, or car chases, can only be a "small film." So they insure their self-fulfilling marketing strategy by refusing to really market it at all. Instead, they save their advertising dollars for the next Schwarzenegger bloodbath.

And this world thinks *Sylvie* is crazy!

The Color Purple

Fading to White

If Steven Spielberg wasn't the most successful director/pro-
ducer in the history of Hollywood, I'd almost feel sorry for
the poor fellow. He has charmed (and obtained millions of
box-office dollars from) much of the movie-going world with
his adventure tales of idealistic boy-children and daring
man-children. The story of his cuddly alien *E.T.* is said to
be the most successful movie of all time. But even millionaire
Hollywood whiz-kids long for respect. And the creator of
Indiana Jones has been too successful for his own good. No
one has taken him seriously as a film *auteur* since *The
Sugarland Express*. It has been suggested that Steven
Spielberg hoped to change all that when he talked Alice
Walker into letting him do the movie of her womanist master-
piece, *The Color Purple*.

But now, poor Steven has learned that ambitious bids
for artistic stature can backfire. His movie of *The Color
Purple* has been out for a while, and it's beginning to look
like Spielberg is not only *not* getting more serious consideration from the film community for this, his most radical
departure in filmmaking, but he is actually being attacked
by all kinds of folks who heretofore ignored his existence.
Ironically enough, although his pursuit of approval seems
to have flopped, he's still a hit at the box office. *The Color
Purple* is doing quite well in theaters across the land.

Doing well while you do damage is nothing new in
Hollywood. I've seen *The Color Purple* twice, and I'd say that
the man with the golden touch has really made a mess of
it this time. I believe that Spielberg genuinely meant well

with his adaptation, but he nonetheless deserves every charge, minus one, being leveled against him. Spielberg's *Purple* has been attacked by (male) black leaders for being racist and anti-male in it's characterization of black men as brutal monsters. It is also reviled by feminists as an act of sabotage against one of our most precious literary works.

Perhaps I'm being naive, but I don't think Steven Spielberg was *trying* to sabotage Walker's novel. He didn't need to try. All he had to do is interpret Alice Walker's material in a way that seemed natural to him. On purpose or not, he has managed to neutralize the feminist power of Walker's narrative and create a frequently racist telling of the remaining story. To cap it off, his distorted vision of this deeply moving novel plum doesn't make sense half the time.

Some of the problems evident in the movie of *The Color Purple* stem from Steven Spielberg's limitations as a filmmaker of the big and the flashy. But, much more than that, the failures of the movie are directly linked to Spielberg's limitations as *white man* glibly attempting to tell the story of a *black woman*. The director's limitations were doubly compounded by his choice of screenwriter (when Alice Walker decided not to take on the job). Menno Meyjes, who wrote the screenplay, is not only, like Spielberg, white and male. He's Dutch.

So we had two white guys, one American, one Dutch, trying to interpret a story about an extended family of southern African-Americans that focuses on one woman's struggle for personal empowerment. Celie survives incest, wife-battering, and separation from her sister Nettie, the one person who gave her unconditional love as a child. She also survives a racist and sexist social system that devalues her first for being black, and secondly for being female, and thirdly for having no access to wealth. Yet the novel, *The Color Purple*, is about more than survival: it is about the triumph of this woman through kinship (mostly sisterhood), and the discovery of self-love, aided by the sexual healing she receives from another woman.

This is out of Spielberg's and Meyjes' league with a vengeance. One wonders what brand of chutzpah made them think they could handle a story like this. And here's the real kicker, how did they think they could tell such a story frankly and fully, and still qualify for a PG-13 rating? It couldn't be done.

I think it was more the need to tone it down and keep it clean than Spielberg's and Meyjes' racial and sexual prejudices that made *The Color Purple* fail. To scrub down Walker's story is to censor it, and Meyjes and Spielberg start censoring from the title credits. Alice Walker's novel opens with the warning "You better not never tell nobody but God. It'd kill your mammy." This is followed by Celie's first letter to God as a pubescent girl trying to make sense of her rape by the man she believes to be her father. Spielberg's story opens like Disney's first technicolor kiddie flick. Celie and her sister Nettie frolic and giggle and play patty-cake in a sea of wildflowers. This idyllic glimpse of childhood is made confusing by our first full-body shot of Celie, who is apparently pregnant. Her father (who *is* verbally abusive) does deliver Walker's opening warning that Celie should "never tell nobody," but he makes his threat when he takes away the baby she has just given birth to.

Showing a father raping his daughter, then choking her when she cries out in fear and pain, and then directly linking that violence with a threat that if she doesn't keep silent her sickly mother will die, and that her death will be on the daughter's head is strong stuff. Too strong for Spielberg. And *way* too potent for censors who want to keep the horrors of family life out of family entertainment. So, instead, Pa delivers the warning where it makes no sense. Is Celie not supposed to tell her mother she had a baby? (Would a mother not notice that one day her daughter is large with child, and the next she is not?) Or maybe she's just not supposed to tell who got rid of it?

By dealing with incest in such a tasteful manner, the filmmakers deny the damage it does, and they confuse the audience. By hiding the violence and terror of the crime from view, they make it harder for us to understand Celie's lack of self-esteem and resistance later in the movie when she is faced by the new brutality of Mister and his children. Having said that, I must admit, in some ways, I am grateful that Spielberg and Meyjes took the hygienic approach. Male filmmakers find it so difficult to portray violence against women in a manner that doesn't consciously or unconsciously glorify it that the method Spielberg took might by a blessing in disguise.

Racism is never a blessing, and the movie *The Color Purple* can be fairly criticized for racism, too. But let's not confuse racism with outraged male pride. When black leaders attack Steven Spielberg for presenting black men as villains, they are, for the most part, off base. Walker's men are also often violent toward the women in their families. That isn't racist, that's reality.

Where Spielberg lets his racism show is in failing to explain black family violence in the context of a racist society. And I don't just mean a kick-the-dog transference. Spielberg never shows us, as Walker does, that the contempt that Mister and Mister's old father show for black women is something they learned from Old Mister's white father, whose rape of a slave woman brought their line into existence. Nor does he explain why young Harpo attacks Celie when Mister brings her home. (He is being loyal to the mother who died in his arms. A fact that Walker makes very clear.)

The brutality of *Purple*'s men, even if not sufficiently explained in the context of racism, is certainly believable. Still, I'm certainly not denying that Spielberg's portrayal of his black male characters is racist. What I'm suggesting is that his racism shows less in the violence of Mister and Harpo, than in their oafishness.

Danny Glover, who plays Mister, is a gifted actor. So much so that he keeps Mister from appearing the total buffoon. But there's no mistaking the ridicule of Spielberg's camera. Look at the way Mister scrabbles around trying to get ready for a date with Shug. He can't dress himself. Later, he can't cook a meal without blowing up the kitchen. And later yet, when he gets together with Shug's husband, he is so ludicrously drunk that the two of them sit around cackling and breaking raw eggs on one another's foreheads.

The movie's portrayal of Harpo is even worse. He falls from rafters and roofs, trips on his own feet, and comports himself like a Stepin Fetchit of old Hollywood. This isn't the character Alice Walker created. *He* was a motherless child, repelled and confused by his father's violence, who felt machismo was what was expected of him, but who eventually rejects male violence and learns to treasure his wife Sophia's strength. Spielberg's Harpo (Willard Pugh) is a stupid fool.

Spielberg is indeed racist in his portrayal of the men of *Purple*. But his racism, is not, as has been claimed, anti-male. For all of their buffoonery, Spielberg makes sure his men are still the power and redemption of the story. The way he and Meyjes manage to bring the men front and center in their rendition of Walker's feminist fable is as crafty a bit of sexist sleight of hand as I've seen in a month of Sundays.

For example, Spielberg orchestrates the movie's most dramatic moment out of nowhere—certainly not out of Walker's novel. Alice Walker creates her Shug as a wonderful wild woman blues singer who, by necessity, leaves her children by Albert to be raised by her parents while she tours the country. The disapproval of both of her parents toward her free-living lifestyle keeps her estranged from them. And she is content to have it so.

Spielberg's Shug (Margaret Avery) is a lost lamb more than a free spirit. She is a woman obsessed with her lost father and the power of paternity. She tells Celie when they first talk that her kids are with her parents because she "never knowed a chile to come out right 'less there's a man around." (Celie tactfully declines to point out that the natural father of Shug's kids, Mister, is known far and wide as a rotten father.) Not having a father-figure around certainly causes Shug grief. She spends much of the movie piteously longing to redeem herself in the eyes of the father who disowned her.

To make the God/Father connections absolutely clear, Shug's father is cast as the local minister. The movie's highest drama occurs when Shug is interrupted in her performance at Harpo's juke-joint by the distant strains of gospel music coming from her father's church. In a production number right out of *Cabin in the Sky*, Shug leads the barroom denizens to her father's church singing the Quincy Jones gospel number, "Maybe God's Trying to Tell You Something." As she marches into the church, toward her stern-faced father on the altar, she moans out the line, "I love you, Lord. Speak to me!" And we know she is pleading with daddy and not Jesus. She is the prodigal daughter begging for male forgiveness. Seldom have I seen a more skillful illustration of the patriarchal great chain of being.

Even Mister, our supposed villain, achieves his own redemption by playing *deus ex machina* in reuniting Celie with her long-lost sister and children. In Walker's version, it is Shug and her young lover Germaine who make waves in the government to try to track Nettie and Celie's children. In the movie, it is Mister who goes to town with money and documentation to save the day. And when the sisters are reunited as middle-aged women to play patty-cake among the flowers again (Spielberg doesn't care how ridiculous his characters look as long as he gets his parallel beginning and end), Mister's silhouette is superimposed across them to insure that you get the point that it was the apologetic old patriarch who provided the happy ending.

Men redeem their daughters and themselves in Spielberg's *Purple*, so despite their violence, they are still in control. To complete the sexist equation, Walker's women have been diminished and divided in the film. Much of their strength and resourcefulness is lost to the viewer. Alice Walker's novel showed us that women with little social power can, through a network of sisterhood that spans time and distance, support and sustain one another. Spielberg shows us how they suffer, but not how they create their own happiness.

Walker's Sophia is part of a clan of Amazon women who look after one another with fierce pride. When their mother's time comes to pass, it is the Amazonian sisters, and not the menfolk of the family, who bear their mother's body to her grave. Spielberg's Sophia (Oprah Winfrey) shines only in her outraged confrontation with Celie when she learns her mother-in-law advised Harpo to beat her. (And we see none of Celie's guilt over this sin against another woman, nor their reconciliation as they make a quilt together.)

Sophia here seems willfully cantankerous. Look at how Spielberg handles the trading of blows between Squeak (Rae Dawn Chong) and Sophia. He creates a comical barroom brawl of it. But does he let us see the women come to peace, caring for one another's children when needed? No. Nor does he show us that Sophia's release from prison to the employ of Miss Millie was a life-saving measure devised by her extended family to get her out of the hell-hole prison that was killing her.

In the novel, it is Squeak, Harpo's lover, who is instrumental in saving Sophia from a prison death. She pleads Sophia's case (pretending that she is out to make life even more miserable for her rival) before her white uncle, the warden. She frees Sophia, at the cost of her own rape.

Hollywood won't show us the sacrifice one woman makes for another. Hollywood invites us, instead, to watch two women slug it out. Spielberg reduces the relationship of Sophia and Squeak to a comical catfight. And when Sophia is released from prison to be Miss Millie's maid, her family is in no way involved. So her servitude to the mayor's wife is completely a symbol of white power instead of a black subversion of that power.

By refusing to tell us about Squeak's rape by her uncle, Spielberg denies her sacrifice and ignores the wide-ranging violence of racism that Alice Walker sets down in her book. Likewise, the film tells us that Celie's pa wasn't really her pa, but it *doesn't* tell us that her real father was lynched for being too successful a black businessman. The only symbol of racism Spielberg allows us is Miss Millie, a spoiled and foolish white *woman*. More cinematic sexism?

Above all, sexism and homophobia are at work in Spielberg's soft-pedaling of the lesbian love story at the center of *The Color Purple*. The relationship between Mister/Albert, Shug, and Celie is the heart of Walker's novel. As a matter of fact, in her essay, "Writing *The Color Purple*," Walker claims that the "germ" of her story came from a bit of gossip related to her by her sister, that in a love triangle they both knew of, "The Wife asked The Other Woman for a pair of her drawers."

The love of Shug is Celie's salvation, it is the blessing she needed to find sexual joy and her own worth. And that same love is the impetus for Mister to mend his ways since it is his physical and emotional brutality against Celie that makes Shug turn away from him. When Celie and Mister make peace with one another in Walker's novel, it is largely through their mutual longing for the singer they think they have both lost. The sexual love between Celie and Shug is essential to Walker's story.

Essential or not, Spielberg doesn't want to consider it. He gives us a chaste kiss and a shot of some wind chimes, and calls it a day. He gives us no indication of the life-long passion and tenderness these two women feel for each other. Showing sexual passion between women is no way to get a PG-13 rating and win the approbation of audiences everywhere, so Steven Spielberg cheats his story.

Spielberg and Meyjes cheat in what they subtract from Alice Walker's novel, and also in what they add. In watching the rich images of *Purple*, the movie, you quickly perceive that E.T.'s creator is more in love with his own technique than the story he tries to tell. He and Meyjes alter Walker's story at will, to their own white, male, politically astute sensibilities. They take out the things they think won't sell, and those aspects of the story they don't like or understand, and they add things that suit their fancy, inappropriate and nonsensical as they might be.

Through the golden haze, the viewer wonders: Why does it snow so much in Georgia (even when the trees are still green)? Why do the children in Mister's and Celie's household (with the exception of Harpo, who ages so much that he seems to get older than his stepmother) never seem to grow up? Why do Celie's children, raised by American teacher/missionary foster parents, not know any English when they meet their birth mother again? What is the point of intercutting the dramatic scene in which Celie almost cuts Mister's through with shots of an African elder performing a scarification ritual on a small boy?

I don't think even Steven Spielberg knew what the point was. If it looked good or sounded good, it went in. And if it didn't suit his interests, it got left out, no matter how essential it was to a rational story line. That's the way it goes when Hollywood gets its mitts on a novel. But it hurts when a novel as righteous as *The Color Purple* is reduced to eye candy.

Whoopi Goldberg, so wonderful in her screen debut as the adult Celie, is catching flack these days from black leaders for saying in publicity interviews that Steven Spielberg was "the only one" who could have made this film. I hope that quote was taken out of context. I don't think Whoopi meant to say that a woman director and/or writer and/or a black filmmaker couldn't have done the *creative* work on this film. I suspect that almost *any* woman or black male could have served the spirit of this novel better in bringing it to the screen.

I think that Ms. Goldberg was simply acknowledging the realities of the marketplace. Only a man of Steven Spielberg's power and wealth would have been allowed to make a movie like this. Only a Steven Spielberg could say to the bigwigs at Warner Brothers, "I want 15 million to make a movie about a black woman's longing for her sister during the first forty years of the century in rural Georgia" and not be laughed off the lot.

So, maybe Steven Spielberg *is* the only man who could have made a movie of *The Color Purple*. But his purple is bleached to white, sanitized, and homogenized for middle-American tastes. The color, and the woman identification, have all but been expunged. Fine performances by a gifted cast cannot completely save it.

With the kind of job he's done, is *this* movie better than *no* movie? It's a tough question, and I'd have to say that as steeped in patriarchal mystique and racism as this movie is, as much as it is an offense against the beauty and power of Alice Walker's novel, it is still preferable to no movie ever being made of this important story. To see a black woman and her family triumph on the American movie screen is almost unheard of. And I'm sure that as muddled and prettied up as this movie is, Alice Walker's message that a poor, battered, and abused woman can find her own worth through the love and support of her sisters of the flesh and spirit isn't completely lost to us. It still, somehow, has a fleeting power to move and inspire. But how much more moving and inspiring it could have been!

Wish You Were Here

The Cries of a Motherless Child

A friend asked me to review this movie. She wanted me to warn women so they wouldn't happen upon the movie unprepared. Unprepared is how *she* had felt, even though she read several reviews of *Wish You Were Here* before going out of her way to see the movie. She resented, she told me, the way the male critics she read had misled her. She felt double-crossed, and I can see why.

The majority of critics called *Wish You Were Here* a "British comedy" about a "spunky," "cheeky" girl. My friend, like many other viewers, entered the theater expecting to see a funny and light-hearted movie. Instead, she felt deeply disturbed by what she saw, and even more disturbed by how the critics had responded to it. "Not *one* review mentioned that there was sexual abuse in the movie!" she told me. Now that I've seen *Wish*, I certainly understand her distress, but I can also understand why the critics didn't warn her about the sexual abuse content. They simply didn't *see* it. The same scene was doubtlessly in both the print my friend saw and the one the reviewers screened. But that scene, and much of the movie, will probably play differently to male and female members of the audience.

Wish You Were Here is the product of David Leland's imagination, a man with a fascination for women's lives, or at least, from all appearances, for the lives of society's "bad girls." Leland started out as an actor before turning his hand to screenwriting. He co-wrote the script for the violent call-girl drama, *Mona Lisa* (1986), and was sole author of the script for this year's *Personal Services*, the "fictionalized" story of a real-life London prostitute turned madam, Cynthia Payne, and her rise to riches.

Interestingly enough, there is some discussion as to whether *Wish* is a prequel to *Personal Services*. Is it the early life of Payne, prior to her entering "the Life?" Leland has denied it. He claims his screenplay is the product of hours of interviews with a variety of women who were teens during the early 50s. Yet he prominently thanks Payne and her biographer in the closing credits of *Wish You Were Here*. Go figure.

No matter whose experience it is based on, Leland's movie is definitely the story of a young woman coming of age during the early 50s. The baby boom years weren't the happiest of times to be reaching womanhood if you wanted anything other than an early marriage and a life of full-time

Lynda (Emily Lloyd), the troubled heroine in Wish You Were Here.

homemaking and motherhood. The upheaval of the war had provided women new freedoms and options, but women's expanding roles contracted again when the boys came home. Women were pushed back into traditional female roles once more, roles that were not to be widely challenged again until the 60s. Yet there have always been, even in the placid 1950s, women who rebelled against playing the dutiful daughter or the self-effacing wife and mother. And, as we all know, the devaluation and exploitation of young girls was around in the 50s. And before. And since.

Leland's heroine, Lynda (Emily Lloyd), is just such a rebel, just such a wounded one. She is a girl at odds with the restrictions and expectations placed upon her, who is nonetheless desperate for male approval and love. Her battle against feminine decorum and for the attention of men begins at an early age. Lynda's personal symbol of male authority and social expectations is, not surprisingly, her emotionally distant father. He is the dominant figure in her young life. Most of who she is and what she does is an act of opposition against her father and, at the same time, a plea for his love. She delights in shocking him and hopes to injure him (even if it is only his social pride) just as he has injured her all of her young life by withholding the kind of acceptance and love she needs.

During her first ten years, the distance between Lynda (as a child, played by Charlotte Ball) and her dad had been as much physical as emotional. She lived as a small child with the mother she loved and a little sister she tolerated without reference to male authority. Her father was off barbering on cruise ships and, later, serving in the wartime Navy. His return home represents the end of her childhood happiness.

This stranger named Hubert (Geoffrey Hutchings) appears one day at her mother's house to claim his place as the center of the household. She is even told to kiss him. Lynda watches for a sign from her mother, but she is too intent on setting up the perfect welcome home tea to notice her daughter's discomfort. Bored with playing the silent little doll in her best dress, Lynda commits her first subversive act. She murmurs "up yer bum" (soon to become her motto) to her little sister. At first the adults respond with a startled silence. Then her outraged father gives her a whack and banishes Lynda to her room.

The war could only intensify from that skirmish. By the summer of Lynda's fifteenth year, when the majority of action in *Wish* takes place, our heroine's relationship with her father is one of all-out guerrilla warfare. Her mother is four years dead. Without her love, approval, and comfort to steady her, Lynda's campaign to outrage her father into paying her attention and giving her love becomes her driving purpose in life. By now, in fact, she seems intent on shocking the entire populace of their stodgy Brighton-ish seaside town.

She rides though town with her skirt hitched to miniskirt length, trying the impress the teenaged boys who loiter there with her Betty Grable gams. She browbeats one conventional lad into going to the movies with her, offering to pay for her own ticket but, although he accepts, he seems genuinely frightened by her boldness and sensuality. It's all an act, of course. But Lynda's blonde beauty and blossoming figure make the act a convincing one. She looks like a woman, but has the emotional vulnerability of the child she still is. It's a dangerous combination. She needs love and attention and has found her developing sexuality doubly useful in her pursuit of it. She can use it to coax some excitement and, more importantly, a little human warmth from the opposite sex. And the flagrant pursuit of that warmth is the kind of rebellious act most likely to enrage her father into taking notice.

Sounds like the perfect recipe for disaster. And it is. Lynda has no better luck with lovers than she has with fathers. First she becomes involved with a bus conductor who spends hours primping and posing in his yellow silk pajamas with a foppish cigarette holder, but less than a minute making love to our virgin heroine. Dave (Jesse

Birdsall) does have the decency to wear a "plonker" (condom) when he prematurely ejaculates, but doesn't have the fortitude to withstand Hubert's angry father routine.

Lynda's second lover has more staying power—with tragic results for her. Eric (Tom Bell) is a friend of her father's, the projectionist at the local movie theater and the town bookie. He is drawn to Lynda's beauty and to her rebellious spirit. She is so full of life, while he is so devoid of it, that like some sort of sexual and spiritual Dracula, he wants to possess her to spark something in himself. Eric knows exactly what he is doing as he stalks his friend's daughter. He begins by spying on her and graduates to feeling her up in the front parlor. Eric is cold and ugly to Lynda even as he tries to wheedle her into sexual submission. He takes every opportunity to remind her that her father doesn't care about her and can't wait to get rid of her. And he makes it equally clear that he is going to hang around her until she gives in.

He takes to loitering outside her back gate at night. Finally, one night when Lynda is filled with despair and rebellion against her father (who has brought his own lover home to her mother's bedroom), she goes out to Eric. She seems willing enough, until the neighborhood bobby discovers them together. At that point, she becomes "scared" and tries to change her mind, but Eric won't let her. "You're not leaving here til you do [it]," he informs her. Then, refusing to wear a condom, he takes her on the floor of the back shed.

Her father, who seemed eager to chase off men closer to Lynda's age, is inexplicably uninterested in protecting his daughter from his lecherous alcoholic pal. He seems glad for an excuse to turn his back on her completely, and Eric's visits to the back shed provide ample reason. Lynda has few options except to go to her older "lover" for shelter and comfort. Shelter, of sorts, he is willing to lend. But as for comfort, Eric is incapable of it. When Lynda, ravaged by her father's rejection and deeply frightened, first comes to him,

49

she begs Eric: "Hold me, please, just hold me." He ignores her cries. As he verbally insults her, he methodically sets about stripping her while she weeps.

Such scenes sound grim and shocking as I have described them. But Leland's version is more ambiguous than mine. Like my friend, I had no doubt that Lynda's and Eric's first sexual coupling was sexual abuse. Moreover, it was rape—and not just in the technical, "statutory" sense. Feminists (and many others) will recognize Eric's relationship with Lynda as sexual exploitation of a minor from beginning to end.

Leland's attitude toward his characters is less easy to gauge. He isn't overtly exploitive in the way he handles his material. Lynda is not portrayed as a Lolita-like nymphet, exactly. The filmmaker's sympathies are certainly with his young heroine. But he is not unsympathetic to Eric or Hubert either. What's a father to do, he invites us to think, when he has a daughter this angry and defiant, this profane and slutty? And as for Eric, he's a tired, unhappy man with a need for a little female companionship. If you find a girl who's ripe for the taking, what's wrong with taking what you can get?

I have plenty of answers to those questions, but I'm not sure Leland does. A filmmaker's impartiality toward his characters may be a good thing, but Leland's attitude goes beyond impartiality. In presenting his story as he does, and concluding it as he does, he seems to be saying that what Lynda experienced was a normal and acceptable rite of passage into womanhood, one that turned out, all in all, for the best.

One way he trivializes the girl's tragedy is by spending much more time showing Lynda's acts of rebellion—her profanity, her sexual curiosity—than in exposing her pain. She seems so resilient and spirited, with her tough talk and that saucy toss of her pretty head, that it's too easy (especially for men) to see her as "spunky" and "cheeky" rather than injured and exploited. It's easy to forget that she is a motherless fifteen-year-old girl crying out for love.

When Lynda jumps on a table at the restaurant where she waitresses to proclaim that she likes "hot willie," it is because her father has just publicly denounced and disowned her and gotten her fired from a job she badly needs. Played for bravado, with a triumphant exit to the applause of the other waitresses and the old woman who plays the piano for the genteel, tea-drinking crowd, Leland invites us to laugh at and treat the scene lightly. He doesn't, for example, show her weeping in the alley behind the restaurant after she marches out the door. He doesn't show her counting out her last shillings, wondering how she's going to live.

It's easier, less distressing, more entertaining, for both Leland and his audience, to see Lynda as a "plucky" young woman who never lets anything get her down for long. Even more damaging, he invites us to view his heroine as a brazen piece of goods whose naive sexuality is an open invitation to (not completely undeserved) exploitation. *Wish* can too easily be seen as a fable about the girl who was asking for it.

And she gets it, Lynda does. From Eric, the "bare-back rider," she gets a pregnancy and a denial of responsibility. From Leland, she receives an even worse betrayal in the way he manipulates his story's conclusion.

Lynda is essentially on her own now. No Eric. No Hubert. No lover. No father. She does receive some friendly support and the address of the local abortionist from a waitress coworker. And she gets some compassionate advice and money from her aunt. (Where was her aunt when she needed her most? Leland doesn't tell us.) Both friend and aunt advise an abortion because they recognize that if she has and keeps her baby, "no one will want to know" her. And it will be like "banging [her] head with a hammer." Lynda recognizes the wisdom of their advice but can't go through with an abortion.

I wouldn't demand abortion as the only possible path for Lynda or her creator to take. There are many ways for a movie to show a teenager's decision to continue her pregnancy in a responsible way. But Leland doesn't use a one of them. He prefers to defy reality in pursuit of a happy ending. First, he doesn't show us *any* of Lynda's pregnancy. He doesn't bother with how she lived or what she went through as an unmarried, pregnant girl in a hostile environment. The way *Wish* plays it, one day Lynda is standing, confused and frightened, outside the door of the abortionist, and the next she is triumphantly returning to town with a beautiful, angelic babe in a shiny new carriage.

Lynda marches through town, head up, looking radiant in a bright yellow frock. The sun shines upon her. She is golden with maternal pride. "Yes, it's mine! All mine!" she proclaims to the shocked but admiring gawkers. She marches to her father's door and rings the bell. The last we see of her she is a shining madonna holding her sweet, perfect little baby up to the sun.

To call such an ending grossly irresponsible is too generous. It is a cheat and a lie, and a dangerous one, to boot. I would never begrudge a child like Lynda, one so betrayed by all the men in her life, her moment of triumph and joy. But fairy tales should always be labeled as such. We, including Leland, know all too well what a grim future faces the undereducated teen mother of an "illegitimate" child who has been rejected by her family. The odds are against her today. They were ten times worse in 1951. She could survive, even triumph, but not without a lot of struggle and suffering.

Yet Leland leaves us with a Lynda who seemingly has not a care in the world. On the one hand he has created a girl who was asking for trouble. Then he has the audacity to suggest that the trouble she gets and deserves (i.e., her pregnancy) is precisely what she needed to make her happy (i.e., it gives her, finally, someone to love who will love her back).

Such an ending is worthy of the right-to-life lobbies at their most romantic and their most evil. It so cheapens

Leland's purpose with this film that it makes you wonder if his intentions were honorable at any point in this haunting story.

David Leland has, with the help of Ian Wilson's photography, produced a visually beautiful film and prompts a stellar debut performance from sixteen-year-old Emily Lloyd. But by focusing on his lead character's sass instead of her pain, and by cheating the reality of the time period he has taken such pains to reproduce, he is false to both his wounded young heroine and the audience who wishes her well.

And as for my male colleagues writing movie reviews, I'd have to agree with my friend. They must not have seen the same movie we did. And if we ever needed (and we don't) proof of how much education is still needed on issues of child sexual abuse, the critical response to *Wish You Were Here* vividly attests to all the work that still needs to be done. Seldom has a "British comedy" left me feeling so depressed.

Streetwise and Seventeen

Teen Movies Tackle a Little Reality

It is impossible to capture the total experience of being a young adult in today's society (or any other, for that matter) in 250 pages or two hours of film. That doesn't keep a lot of people from trying. The coming-of-age novel and the teen movie are two of the most enduring formulas in American culture.

Most coming-of-age novels are, of course, written for adults, by adults. The author seeks to sort through the *mishegaas* of her (or, usually, his) past in a way that will elicit bittersweet recognition and memories in the adult reader. Teen movies are a little different. True, the *auteurs* are still chronologically adult, but they are not aiming for an adult market. The target audience for teen movies (indeed, *most* movies) is teenagers, not adults. The reason is simple: young adults represent the majority of the audience for feature films.

Documentary films are usually another matter. While Hollywood produces other-world adventures, nauseatingly naughty sex comedies, and slash-n-trash horror flicks for the young, it is usually adults who are drawn to the starkness of nonfiction film. We love to have our worst fears realized, to consume culture we can claim as enlightening and educating (not to mention depressing). Recently two feature-length documentaries, *Seventeen* and *Streetwise*, represent a harsher but more believable kind of teen movie.

Seventeen wasn't originally meant to be a feature-length film; it was commissioned to be part of the "Middletown" documentary series shown on PBS. But the powerful film produced by the wife-and-husband team Joel DeMott and Jeff Kreines was refused an airing on public television. And, despite the cries of censorship, I can't imagine anyone thinking that such a film *would* be allowed on general-access TV. Content aside, the slang dialect spoken by the teen characters of the film is extremely scatological. There are enough obscenities in this film to sink a battleship—or at least to make the sailors thereupon feel right at home.

Seventeen's central figure is a young woman named Lynn Massie. She lives at home with her mother, father, and younger brother. She attends Central High in Muncie, Indiana. So far, it all sounds very "normal" (to borrow a term from the *Globe*) and wholesome. Wholesome it ain't, but there is a frenzied normalcy about Lynn and her family and friends. Everyone we see has trouble relating to the struggles of life and to each other. Lynn is suffering all the timeless agonies of being a seventeen-year-old girl. She is filled with rage and resentment against her parents and she has an unveiled contempt for her school. And then there is boy trouble, of which Lynn has a most tormenting variety. Her boyfriend suffers her endearments and uses her for casual entertainment, but he doesn't seem to love or even like her. A classic situation—and Lynn is white, John black.

Filmmakers DeMott and Kreines provide ample proof that interracial relationships remain painful and sometimes explosive. Like Juliet (or Maria), Lynn gets no comfort from either camp. She berates John for his indifference, saying that white girls "swallow our pride for you guys," and that white guys won't touch cross-dating white girls.

If she overstates the case, it is clear that interracial dating makes a lot of people unhappy. Lynn's mother is philosophical until a cross is burned on their front lawn. Soon thereafter the Massies start receiving threatening phone calls that Lynn claims come from young black women resentful of whites romancing black guys. She is even preached at by black male friends who assure her that John only wants "fuck [her] over."

Seventeen graphically shows us a racism that is seldom subtle or well-mannered. Among these working people who live and struggle side by side, racism is a raw and constant wound. It is yet another source of anger and fear in lives that know too much of both.

Seventeen expresses well the kind of helpless rebellion of the young and working-class. Perhaps it expresses it too well; we see Lynn and her contemporaries only when they are acting out. We see them smoke, drink, carouse, fight, and do dope, but we don't see them sewing their prom dresses or enjoying cokes together after a movie. Lynn, for example, is shown as consistently foul-mouthed and in conflict. We know she must have a job as a waitress because we see about five seconds of film wherein she places condiments on a plate of food, but we never see her talking to her boss or waiting on a customer. Nor do we see (with the exception of one endearing scene of boytalk at bedtime) other aspects of her everyday life that would place her angst in context.

Manipulating reality to suit a viewpoint or theme is one of the age-old problems of documentary. *Seventeen* suffers from this and another aesthetic problem common to "direct cinema" or "cinema verité." We see a grainy image at best, and, at worst, deep shadow or darkness, with the dialogue muffled or lost in a cacophony of background noises.

Another recent documentary about youth has none of the technical problems of *Seventeen*. In fact, *Streetwise* could easily be accused of being too slick as it chronicles the lives of the young street people of Seattle. Most of the characters we meet in *Streetwise* are even younger than Lynn Massie, and face an even more desperate life.

These are the youngsters who panhandle, deal dope, pimp, and prostitute along Seattle's Pike Street. The film, directed and shot by Martin Bell and based on the words and still photographs of co-filmmakers Cheryl McCall and Mary Ellen Mark, is a very ambitious one. Unlike *Seventeen*, *Streetwise* doesn't focus on a single teen; there is no one protagonist. We see vignettes of over a dozen young lives and sometimes it is difficult to keep everyone straight without a proverbial scorecard—or at least an omniscient narrator.

But despite the occasional confusion, the filmmakers were wise to avoid a narrator, that adult voice who keeps everything tidy and clear. They were wise to avoid, as much as possible, the voices of adults altogether. These kids tell their own stories of poverty, sexual abuse, and neglect with a calm that is heartbreaking. Heartbreaking, too, are the dreams of wealth and happy family life of these children who "date" seventy-year-old men and get their meals out of "regs" (garbage dumpsters they visit daily).

Most of these kids are not, however, homeless. Tiny, one of a trio of youngsters we see a good deal of, is a fourteen-year-old prostitute who lives with her mother, a greasy-spoon counter waitress and an acknowledged alcoholic. Tiny's mother is so filled with despair and beer that she can spare little concern for her daughter's life. She deludes herself that the prostitution is a "phase that [Tiny's] going through" because of the needed money it provides. She tells us that waitresses make very little and shares the wonderment she felt the first time Tiny brought home $200 for a day of tricks.

But if the filmmakers are honest about the fact that most of these kids still have ties to their troubled families, they are less than honest about their interrelationships and the trades they ply to survive. I have since read that several of the older teens portrayed as protective older-kids-on-the-block are actually pimps for some of the younger characters. If true, this is a troubling omission, and an aspect of the story worthy of explication.

In fact, Bell, Mark, and McCall often keep important aspects of the story from the viewer, either by design or chance, point of view or time constraint. In terms of slant, *Streetwise* has the opposite problem of *Seventeen*. While we see little of a positive or a tender nature in the life of Lynn Massie, the lives of Tiny and her boyfriend, Rat, are almost too attractive. We see them laughing, roller-skating, snuggling with a puppy, so it is an orchestrated shock when we see Rat gnaw at a chicken wing he has pulled from a dumpster. It may be a blessing that we never see Tiny with a john; but in the case of another youngster, DeWayne, we are shown so little of his despair that his suicide, the shocking climax to the film, is totally unexpected and jarring.

Streetwise is a beautifully photographed film, brilliantly edited by Nancy Baker. If it fails in telling the whole story fairly, it is probably only because the filmmakers have taken on too much in their attempt to capture the broken lives of a score of young survivors in two hours. After all, capturing even one life in two hours just isn't possible.

But, flawed as these two films are, they are fascinating and important to see. These are teen movies in a sense that *Beach Blanket Bingo* and *Porky's* (or even *Rebel Without a Cause*) can't even approach. Still, I suspect that most teens (and most adults) would rather see one of Hollywood's horny farces over either of these films. And who could blame them? Unlike the synthetic heroines of Hollywood, Lynn and Tiny aren't easy to forget. *Seventeen* and *Streetwise* are movies that haunt your dreams and make you hunger for a day when all that anger and hope fuel a process of change for all the Tinys of the world.

Serious Thoughts
About the Lighter Side

Adventures in Babysitting

Afraid of the Dark

I don't need to tell you that the Hollywood film is now, and always has been, elitist and racist (not to mention sexist and homophobic). We can all trot out our favorite examples of our least favorite -ism as presented in American film. The examples are legion and represent incontrovertible proof of how insidiously nasty a jolly little movie can be.

There is, however, a difference in the *form* of the racism, classism, etc. over the years. In the 50s or 60s, the sins were largely those of omission. It wasn't so much that minorities and working people were portrayed *badly* as that they weren't portrayed *at all*. Sure, there were Stepin Fetchits and Dead End Kids of the 30s; but throughout most movie history, poor folks and people of color simply didn't exist.

Today it's a little more complicated. There is more diversity in the people presented on film. More and more often, black or gay or strong female or blue- or pink-collar characters appear in American movies. It's *how* we are portrayed that continues to be a problem. And it's a monster of a problem. For target practice this time out, I offer you *Adventures in Babysitting*, a film that could convince anyone that invisibility isn't so bad after all.

As the ads state, this is a film about "three normal kids and one dependable babysitter." A normalcy of sorts may thrive in the prosperous and very white west suburbs of Chicago, but common sense and self-reliance do not. And neither does human sensitivity toward others in WASP-dominated society. At least not in the Chicago 'burbs with the young people presented by writer David Simkins and director Chris Columbus.

As the movie begins, our babysitter, Chris Parker (Elisabeth Shue) doesn't want to be a babysitter. As a senior in high school, she considers herself too old and sophisticated for such a menial occupation. She'd like to be out celebrating her anniversary with her steady, Mike (Bradley Whitford), but he claims that there is a sickness at home and cancels on her. We know the guy is a real oinker (when he snows the downcast Chris with "Girls like you come along once in a lifetime," the young women sitting behind me yelled, "Blecch—drop dead!"), but Chris is duped by his flashy charm. Her romantic hopes for the evening dashed, she agrees to help out a frantic couple scheduled to attend a high-class do.

The Andersons (what else could they be called?) live in a palatial yet tasteful house with their two children, Brad and Sara. The sittee is young Sara (Maia Brewton), a spunky young girl obsessed with her favorite comic hero, "The Mighty Thor." Brad (Keith Coogan) is a good-natured, seemingly intelligent pubescent boy. Clearly *he* should be watching his sister for the evening, but he has his own plans to spend the night with his friend, a noisome kid named Daryl (Anthony Rapp). He also has a major crush on Chris. So when he finds out who the sitter is, he decides to stay home.

In an upscale neighborhood like this, the biggest excitement Chris and the kids expect is a run for ice cream at Haagen Dazs (no HoJo's or Tastee-Freez for these yuppups). But complications quickly arise. Chris's best friend, a haughty drip who runs away from home only to chicken out at a Chicago bus terminal, calls for help. She has taken a taxi to the city, and without cab fare for the return trip she is totally at a loss as to how to get home again. She whines for Chris to rescue her from the big, bad city.

What is a dependable Breck girl to do? She can't just abandon her friend to her bitter fate. Yet she knows that no responsible (white) sitter would take a (white) child into the (black) city after dark. She moans that the Anderson parents would "die if they knew I took you into the city!" The three kids refuse to stay behind, so all four pile into Chris's mom's station wagon and head for the urban wasteland.

If *Adventures in Babysitting* had, at any point, counteracted the mythology of suburban, white paranoia, this movie might have been bearable, even fun to watch. Of course, it does not. This teen comedy-adventure movie reinforces every nightmarish fear the middle class have of the urban poor.

First the kids have a tire blow out on the freeway and are rescued by a Captain Kidd tow-rig driver with a claw hand. Hence, the kids' (and our) first lesson is to fear the disabled. For while Handsome John is a merciful pirate, he is also a madman. When he gets a CB tip that his wife is cheating on him, he hijacks the kids to his home, pulls out his shotgun, and starts shooting.

Our heroes scramble for cover in a car which is, at that moment, being stolen by a black thief. Joe Gipp (Calvin Levels) is, like Handsome John, fundamentally a sympathetic character. But does he let the kids out of the car? No. He takes them to the chop-shop headquarters where the head thug decides they've seen too much and must be eliminated. Chris and her charges escape (with a *Playboy* containing mob information—don't ask!) and the rest of the movie consists of bad guys (white bossman, beefy black enforcer, and Joe Gipp, the driver) chasing the frightened kids through the dark, foggy filth of Chi-town.

Meanwhile, back at the bus terminal, poor Brenda (Penelope Ann Miller) is having it rough. A vendor refuses to take a check for a hot dog, and she has her glasses lifted by a homeless woman, mistakes a sewer rat for a kitten, sees a gun-flashing hobo at every turn, and generally has a miserable time of it. And if anyone deserved a little misery, it's our Brenda. This young woman, like so many Ugly Americans, blithely believes that the world exists for her comfort. Other people's more fundamental needs are beneath her consideration. Early on, a shabbily dressed old man bangs on the door of the station phone booth while Brenda is making a call. "Get out of my home!" he yells. "You just moved!" she shouts back, as she kicks his belongings from the booth. Since the filmmakers play the scene for big laughs, you can only assume that they are giving us another little lesson in contempt for the poor and homeless.

Brenda is an elitist brat. Chris, our golden-girl heroine, isn't much better. Although, well-bred child that she is, Chris is always *polite* to the less fortunates she encounters, her air of condescension is so thick you could cut it with a knife. The moral here is not that if you treat people with respect and compassion you might get some of those positive emotions back. Instead, the manifest message is that if you are young, attractive, white, and upper-class, others should treat you with admiration and respect, and *will*. (Or, if they don't, they may be dismissed as bad people who will suffer for their violation of the social code.)

Consider the scene wherein Chris and the kids duck through an alley door to avoid the baddies and find themselves on stage with Chicago blues great Albert Collins. Chris apologizes for interrupting their "little concert," but when she and the kids try to leave the stage, Mr. Collins tells them that "nobody gets outta here without singing the blues." So Chris begins a litany of complaints ("It's so hard, babysitting these guys...") which is soon put to a blues riff by the sidemen. By the end of her "number," the place is rocking. The entire black audience is enchanted with Chris's soul. They completely relate to her tale of woe. Natch! As Chris and her pals leave amid embraces and high-fives from the club's customers, I could almost hear the filmmakers congratulating themselves for creating such a liberal scene.

After all, the black characters are *nice* to the kids, aren't they? There is goodwill all around, isn't there? Yes, it all *sounds* lovely, but it *feels* just like the massah's chillun going down to the slave quarters to charm Uncle Tom and all the other black folk. With a soundtrack featuring Collins, the exquisite Koko Taylor, and, fleetingly, Muddy Waters, a black audience going into ecstasy over Chris's white rap is an incredible insult.

And so it goes. When *Adventures in Babysitting* isn't promoting fear and hatred of blacks and Hispanics, it is promoting an image of them as docile children eager to serve and support owning-class whites. I recall only one non-white professional, an East Indian emergency room doctor who is benign but stupid. There is no winning with this movie.

Where racism and classism are the order, can sexism be far behind? I went to see this film because of its unusual title concept: a teen adventure film with a female lead, satirically based in the ultimate teengirl caregiver stereotype. A babysitter as a swashbucking hero sounds great. If only it were.

Despite the misleading poster for the movie, Chris is no swashbuckler. She's not even a Supermom figure. She spends most of her time standing around looking cute and acting bemused or frightened. When push comes to shove, Chris keeps her hands to herself. When the kids get caught in the middle of a gang war, or when Chris spots the cheating boyfriend with an "easy chick," Chris allows young Brad and Daryl, in clear violation of her role as surrogate parent, to act as her protectors.

Chris's one flash of glory comes during the gang war, when Brad's defense of her honor gets him a knife in the foot from one of the gang leaders (one gang leader is Hispanic, the rival gang's leader is black). The hoodlum proudly threatens, "You don't fuck with the Lords of Hell!" Chris responds by grabbing the knife from Brad's shoe and bellowing, "You don't fuck with the babysitter."

It's funny and endearing for the moment, but, on reflection, it seems far too impersonal, almost passive. Why not, "You don't fuck with me!" or "You don't fuck with us, either!'"? Chris speaks from her belatedly protective feelings as a female caregiver, and it patently dilutes the power of her action.

If there is a heroic female figure in the film, it is young Sara, who is brave and strong—even if she does pattern herself on an Aryan male superhero. It is through her that the filmmakers make their greatest play for our fear and hatred. In the movie's climax, Sara is stalked through a high rise under construction by the mob enforcer—a small white girl stalked by a large, mean black man. Sara triumphs, of course. In fact, the movie's final gag (which follows the closing credits) is a shot of the black enforcer, forgotten and left clinging to the side of a building, fifty stories up. He is whimpering. Very funny.

But the *real* hero of *Adventures in Babysitting* isn't female. He is young Brad Anderson, who comes of age during a dangerous night of serving the golden princess he loves but cannot possess. It's all very sweetly male-mythic, depressing for anyone expecting the rite of passage to be that of a courageous young woman.

Chris, our title hero, changes very little during the course of action. Sure, she dumps her rotten boyfriend, but she picks another up at a University of Chicago frat party. But then, why should she change? Golden girls don't need a transformation; they're already perfect.

I'm sure that the people who made this film, if they thought about it at all, believe that they made a funny, friendly movie that meant no harm to anyone. When the media talks about the "new racism" (a stupid term if ever there was one), they are usually referring to those ever-increasing outbursts of overt white supremacy in action. Events like those in Forsyth County and Howard Beach are indeed frightening, but I suspect that movies like *Adventures in Babysitting* do far more damage. They feed on the more covert racist (elitist, sexist) impulses of the "liberal" white majority. They teach white middle class suburban kids a lesson they surely don't need: to fear the dark, the different, couple that fear with contempt.

If I were able to tell David Simkins and Chris Columbus what I've just told you, they'd probably dismiss my concerns with a glib protestation of their good intentions and fair-minded attitude toward everyone. They just wouldn't get it. And *that* is the scariest part of all.

Wildcats

A Feminist Football Fable?

Let me first confess that I don't like football. No, I take that back. I hate football. We all know about the purposeful violence, the unnecessary brutality of it. Every time I see a crushing tackle I think of Darryl Stingley (a New England Patriot made a quadriplegic by one killer play) and am reminded that football is a gladiator game in which a white owner has a white coach tell a white quarterback to instigate a play in which black players attempt to maim one another for fun and profit.

Therefore, I was probably not the best person to review the Goldie Hawn film, *Wildcats*, in which Hawn tackles football. Yet I must admit to being attracted to a movie invariably labeled in reviews both positive and negative, "a feminist fantasy." I wanted to see for myself just what a feminist fantasy looks like.

The title sequence sets the scene. We see home movies wherein a tiny golden girl idolizes her crewcut football-coach father. She has a football theme birthday cake. And for Christmas, when her older sister is thrilling over the gift of an angel doll, the elfin blonde is transported by a new football helmet.

The movie itself opens with Molly McGrath (Goldie Hawn) in full football regalia hamming it up for her sister Verna's camera. They are taking gag photos for the year-book of the prosperous suburban Chicago high school where Molly toils, with so little recognition, in the athletic department. She bemoans the fact that she may be stuck coaching women's track all her life. (At which point I wanted to shout,

"What's wrong with women's track? Valerie Brisco-Hooks is worth ten Jim McMahons any day!") But her big break may have finally arrived. The junior varsity football coach has fallen ill, and Molly dreams of being his replacement.

Molly is fully cognizant of the sexist attitudes of the principal and, especially, the school's athletic director, Dan Darwell (Bruce McGill, playing macho villainy to the hilt). When her sister encourages her with the tired maxim that the worst he can do is say no, Molly corrects her. "He could say, 'No, Babes'," she points out.

His reaction, especially after Molly has the bad judgment to beat him at racquetball, is even worse. The JV job goes to the effeminate but male home ec teacher. As a taunt, Darwell offers her a varsity coaching job. The catch is that the job is at a ghetto school and the mostly black team has won only one game last season—when the opposing team's bus broke down.

In a noble moment of macha bravada, Molly takes the job. "I'll show you tough!" she proclaims, as she strikes off for the urban wasteland. At Central High she finds the dingy halls patrolled by Dobermans and meets the careworn but still caring Principal Edwards (played nicely by Nipsy Russell). Meeting her team is more distressing. They start by exposing their genitals to her en masse, and individually they curse her and fart in her face.

Molly is just about beaten by their harsh resistance to her coaching. But when they trash her office, spray paint "Get Out Pussy!" on her walls, and break the stopwatch given her by her sister and two daughters, she fights back. She challenges the team to an athletic contest, and wins them over with her prowess.

Soon thereafter, we are treated to the moral of the movie. In a scene with her two daughters, Molly explains why she must continue on her seemingly masochistic course. "You can be anything you want to be," Molly assures her children. Even, as the youngest hopes, a helicopter pilot. But the skepticism of the elder daughter (Robyn

Lively) seems more realistic than Mom's determined optimism. After all, if a woman can be anything she wants to be, why isn't Molly a star quarterback instead of a beleaguered coach?

I can't help worrying that when you show a woman hero who so desperately wants to buy into the macho mystique you only trivialize the *real* struggles of women against sexism. Of course, fighting for a livable wage or for decent child care—worries that Molly McGuire doesn't seem to have—is not the stuff of comedy.

If screenwriter Ezra Sacks's view of sexism is a little simplistic, his view of racism is a complete blank. Couldn't part of the players' resentment come from the fact that their new coach is not only a "pussy," but a white one at that? She is, after all, another Great White Hope who can create a winning team out of a band of losing hoodlums, and a school with spirit and pride out of an apathetic armed camp. In a complete flight into Cloud Cuckooland, there is no racial tension at Central High—or even among the players from Central and their white suburban rivals.

It could be argued that in showing us a world where race is not an issue, the filmmakers were not only keeping it light but also providing a positive model. But it sure looks like a cop-out when Molly blithely wanders through the ghetto searching for a truant quarterback and ends up offering three black men from a pool hall a ride in her van with no apparent recognition on her part of the possible danger of the situation. (Good golly, Miss Molly! That scenario would be fraught with unpleasant possibilities whether the men were black, white, or charteuse!)

In another scene, villain Darwell brings allegations to Principal Edwards that several of his star players do not meet academic requirements for play. Having seen the players buying term papers off the mercenary school egghead (Tab Thacker), we believe Darwell's charges. Do Edwards and Coach McGrath start a tutoring program for their beloved players? No way. Edwards throws Darwell out of the school and Central's coach and principal continue to ignore the problem of the high school athlete who fails to get an education while he "kicks ass" for the glory of his school.

As always, I expect that I am asking too much from *Wildcats*. It does have a few mildly comical moments that are not based on cruelty. I must admit that I loved Central's cheerleaders, a funky troupe in T-shirts, shorts, and sweatpants who do a truly great cheer entitled "You Ugly! Yeahhhh—You Ugly!" which beats the taffy out of the mild-mannered "Ashes to Ashes" cheer the sweet young things at my high school used to do.

And Hawn is both strong and vulnerable as she fights sexist villainy on the playing field and at home, where her bland bad guy of an ex-husband threatens to take away her children if she doesn't give up her dream. There is little doubt that she has the part of the plucky heroine perfected, even if she has become a little too sincere and serious for her own comedic good.

Many of the supporting actors threaten to outshine the star. Swoosie Kurtz is notable among them as Molly's sister, Verna. In a throwaway part meant to provide a prop for Hawn, Kurtz manages an understated yet thoroughly engaging performance, one that makes you wish Hollywood would be smart enough to give this woman a lead role once in a while.

Wildcats is generally a likable film, especially recommended for women who like football. For the rest of us, the triumph of a pack of underdogs is always heartwarming, particularly when they are led by a woman who, faced by oppression both at home and on the job, kicks some male ass—and wins.

Who's That Girl

Who's That Madonna?

Let's be clear about one thing straight off: If you are not fascinated (or at least intrigued) by the show business phenomenon known as Madonna, you shouldn't bother to see her latest movie, *Who's That Girl*. If you like screwball comedy, you *might* like it anyway, but there are certainly scores of screwball comedies with more flair and substance than this one—*Bringing Up Baby*, for instance. It's obvious that screenwriters Andrew Smith and Ken Finkelman stole most of their material from that definitive screwball classic of 1938, which featured Katharine Hepburn and Cary Grant falling in love as they rushed from disaster to disaster in pursuit of a missing dinosaur bone and a music-loving leopard. *Bringing Up Baby* is hard to improve upon, and *Who's That Girl* doesn't even come close. Really, Madonna is *the* draw of this film. If you don't see what the big deal is with this pop superstar, then stay clear of this movie.

I think I know what the big deal is with Madonna, but I'm not sure how comfortable I am with it. Madonna, both as a pop singer and more recently as a movie star, is an amazing amalgamation of all the conflicting images and choices of the American woman—in suitably exaggerated form. Now that she has abandoned her earlier look of black lace, twenty pounds of baubles, and crucifixes hanging from her ears, she looks like a throwback to 50s glamour. But Madonna is very much an 80s woman—tough, and very conscious of her needs and desires.

Feminists, myself included, are frequently dismayed by the packaging of this talented (yes, I *do* believe she's talented)

71

woman as the new rock/Hollywood sex goddess. In her concerts, rock videos, and movies, she is usually portrayed as an unrepentant sex kitten, a platinum blonde in black leather and fishnet stockings. The music video for her "Open Your Heart" makes the most blatant use of this image. She plays an exotic dancer in a dominatrix push-up bodysuit with twirling gold pasties at the points of her black leather-clad breasts. Yet, at the close of that same video, she literally skips out on her peep-show job with a small boy in tow (he could be her son, brother, mirror image, or just an adoring fan). As she runs away from the angry male peep-show manager she displays no fear, only a blithe contempt. She is dressed in a baggy gray suit and homburg, the sex object turned androgyne.

That same androgyne figure appears in the music video for the title song of *Who's That Girl.* The gray-suited imp watches the movie's heroine, Nikki Finn, in a variety of action sequences while Madonna sings a love song about how compelling and beautiful "that girl" is. The singer is, of course, singing a love song to *herself*—something no one but Madonna would have the nerve to do.

There you have the essence of Madonna. One minute she is a harsh sex goddess, the next a streetwise tomboy or a shy, homesick child who transforms herself into a flamenco vamp. But above all she is a chameleon with her eye on the main chance. She is a woman who wants it all, and knows how to get it. And she couldn't care less whether feminists or right-wing parents approve of her methods. When the high road and the bottom line diverge, we know whither goest Madonna. When living in a material world, she has told us, you should always be a material girl.

Those who think of Madonna's blonde bombshell persona as a Marilyn Monroe, a little girl lost in desperate need of finding herself through male approval, are, I think, missing the point. Although she will do anything, play any role or fantasy, to get what she wants, Madonna-the-image (and very possibly the woman behind the image) doesn't lack identity. She knows who she is, and (as we see in the "Who's That Girl" video) she loves herself. She just doesn't mind manipulating her appearance and actions to better manipulate others—especially men, with their money and power.

While Marilyn was often portrayed as a gold digger, she was always a gold digger with a heart of 14K. In the end, Marilyn was always a slave to her feminine, loving heart. Madonna is a slave to no one, and regardless of the lyrics she sings, she loves no one but her Self. Once you begin to understand the image of Madonna, you can easily understand why *Who's That Girl* doesn't feel like a standard screwball comedy, and therefore seems less successful as such.

Here's a basic rundown of the plot: Madonna is Nikki Finn, a punk Betty Boop released from prison after serving four years for the murder of her small-time hood boyfriend. She was framed. She is innocent of murder ("Hey, I liked Johnny, but not enough to kill him"), but by no means innocent. She is a light-fingered wildwoman. She takes anything she can lay hands on and can total a luxury car better than any queen of the demolition derby.

Griffin Dunne plays tax attorney Loudon Trott, a buttoned-down, status-conscious fellow about to make his big move by marrying the boss's daughter and moving into a high-class Manhattan co-op. Trott's boss, Simon Worthington (John McMartin), is portrayed as a WASP psychopath who is as ruthless in personal matters as he is in business. He makes Trott sign a detailed prenuptial agreement with his daughter ("Someday...*none* of this will be yours") and browbeats his docile son-in-law-to-be into picking up a rare Patagonian *felix congola* (it looked like the Mercury cougar mascot to me) at the docks and Nikki at the prison gates. He is supposed to deliver Nikki to the bus station and the nearly extinct kitty to multimillionaire Montgomery Bell (Sir John Mills).

In her zany togs (my favorite outfit was a black patent leather leotard under a white tutu, topped by a motorcycle jacket and accessorized with a monkey-face purse and Beatle boots), Nikki is far and away the most dangerous of the rare caged cats on the loose. In less than a day she makes mincemeat of Loudon's ordered path to success. She means no harm, not to Loudon, anyway. But she's not going home to Philly before she clears her name in New York.

Trott spends the first two-thirds of the movie suffering numerous indignities, and cursing Nikki for her dishonesty and disregard for property and social etiquette. At one point he turns to her and says, "I just want to know: Are you the Anti-Christ?" Then, abruptly, magically, in the last third of the film he falls in love with Nikki. He becomes thankful for the upheaval her particular brand of *joie de vivre* brings to his staid existence. Despite the violence and terror of the day he spends trailing her around New York, he sees their time together as "the greatest day of my life." And he runs off with her at the end of the movie.

Now this is all externally a *very* predictable representation of the standard screwball plot. And one of the reasons women are drawn to the screwball comedy is its portrayal of the female lead as liberator. Cary Grant, Ryan O'Neal (in *What's Up, Doc?*, 1972), Jeff Daniels (in *Something Wild*, 1986), and dear, hapless Griffin all needed the love of a looney-tune woman to bring them to their true liberated selves. They needed to loosen up and live life closer to the edge—and Kate Hepburn, Barbra Streisand, Melanie Griffith, and Madonna are just the women to force them to do it.

There is something very satisfying in this unusual Hollywood archetype. Too often it is men who give women their identity and freedom in movieland. In the screwball comedy the opposite is true. But there is a downside to the woman-as-liberator image, too. First, all of these women are ditzes who aren't safe to cross the street by themselves (although it is almost always their male escorts who come to harm, not the women). Moreover, it is easy to see the woman-as-liberator as very much a male fantasy. Every guy is looking for a reckless beauty who'll awaken his sexuality and do things good girls wouldn't even dream about. The male sexual fantasy aspect of the screwball plot is, not surprisingly, much less obvious in the 30s classics than in recent variations on the theme, like *Something Wild*. The most unsettling of all the between-the-lines messages in screwball movies is that the oppressed are actually the liberated. Women don't need to fight for their rights, Hollywood seems to be saying, because they are already the only truly free people on earth.

This merriest of movie formulas has yet another gloomy aspect for the feminist viewer. In the traditional screwball comedy, the female lead's wackiness and apparent liberation are based not on her sense of self-worth and independence, but rather on her obsessive love-at-first-sight for the male lead. *Who's That Girl* lacks this obsessive love; its screenwriters sacrificed the demands of the screwball formula in the service of the Madonna mystique, the key to which is her unwavering self-absorption. How can you stay true to such an image within the romantic construct of the screwball comedy? You can't.

In classic screwball, the woman is *really* chasing the man (even if she pretends to be chasing a cat or a suitcase). Madonna, on the other hand, is really chasing the bad guys, so as to clear her name. She liked her old lover, but not enough to kill him. And she likes Loudon Trott, but not enough to love him—that is, not enough to become selfless. Look at the scene in a mock jungle after Trott has been transmogrified into adoring Nikki. When the two consummate their sexual attraction, at no point does Nikki express anything more than simple horniness over being without heterosexual lovemaking for four years. She doesn't say, "I love you." She says, "It's been a long time." Similarly, when Nikki breaks up the marriage of Loudon to Wendy Worthington (Haviland Morris) in the final scene, she does not say, "Stop this marriage because I love the groom." She says, "Stop—the groom is in love with *me*." Those who criticize the lack of chemistry between Dunne and Madonna should remember that there is a simple reason for it: Both principals are in love with the same person.

From start to finish, *Who's That Girl* is the story of a woman in love with herself, whose motivation is at all times geared toward her own survival and, beyond that, to her own joy and comfort. Since I was raised a good Italian-American Catholic girl, the message of Madonna and *Who's That Girl* doesn't set easily on my soul. But Madonna Louise Ciccone was also born Italian-American and Catholic. When she was six her mother died, and she was left the oldest daughter in a family of six children. In a recent interview with Jane Pauley, Madonna recalled that time in her life, saying she decided that if she couldn't have her mother, she would be strong and take care of herself. She has done just that. And although she has had her share of rotten work and love relationships with men, I honestly believe that, since the age of six, Madonna Ciccone has never faltered in her determination to take care of herself, to be strong, and to get what she wants out of life.

It horrifies me to think of the damage Madonna did, and continues to do, with the song and video "Papa Don't Preach" (in which a pregnant teen tells her father—in a litany—that "I'm keeping my baby-oh, I'm gonna keep my baby!"). I recently heard that it was the most popular rock video *worldwide* in 1986. But I can't bring myself to vilify the overall message of Madonna, either as rock star or movie star in *Who's That Girl.* I want women to be strong *and* compassionate, to take care of themselves, yet deeply care for others. But maybe in a world that still teaches women to lose themselves in love and to sacrifice themselves for God and family, an extreme role model like Madonna, with her disrespect for authority, her fearlessness, and her self-centeredness, isn't the worst image for young girls to see. Those ingredients may not make for a suitably romantic heroine or for a successful screwball comedy, but Madonna's movie sure beats the sweet, docile "you are my everything, I am your doormat" approach of the women pop singers and movie stars of my youth.

Whoopi Goldberg

Watching Hollywood Make Whoopi...Fail

I had wanted to review Whoopi Goldberg's movie, *Fatal Beauty*. I didn't, because I never got a chance to see it. It opened and closed in a flash, to prevailingly rotten reviews a few months back. So why bring it up now? Because Whoopi Goldberg's latest movie, *The Telephone*, which was screened for a few critics recently (again to really rotten reviews), disappeared without even opening. It looks like Whoopi Goldberg is well on her way to becoming box office poison. And, in my opinion, little to none of the blame is Goldberg's. Despite the humongus investment of time and money in each of Goldberg's films to date, it begins to look more and more like Hollywood is doing its best to ruin the career of this gifted actor. They may just succeed, too.

Whoopi Goldberg is no instant star. She has been working at the craft of acting and the creation of character for a lot of years. According to various profiles and interviews, she grew up poor in a New York City housing project and has been acting since the age of eight. Like a lot of us, she experienced the turmoil of the 60s and 70s first-hand. She was married for a time, had a daughter, struggled with drug abuse (and won), and did what she had to do to support her daughter and herself while she tried to make it as a performer. Much has been made in the media about the fact that she was a "welfare mother." But she was also, from what I have read, everything from a bricklayer to a licensed cosmetician doing mortuary work before she hit it big.

All of that experience went into her theater work and her stand-up comedy act. She created an irresistible cluster of fascinating female characters. They include a "Surfer Chick," a junkie named Fontaine, a Jamaican housekeeper, a Little Black Girl who fantasizes about having blonde hair, and a woman with severe physical disabilities who is about to be married. These women Whoopi Goldberg created for her one-woman show are like nothing any of us had ever seen before. And, once seen, these fully realized characters are not forgotten. Goldberg's caring and respectful vision of these women, while not always uncontroversial, is clearly informed by a deep social conscience. Through them, Whoopi attacks cultural and economic racism, ableism, and sexism. Even a character like the Surfer Chick, who you would expect to be simply a privileged Valley Girl, turns out to have lessons to share about the horrors of teen pregnancy.

It was this band of female characters that brought Whoopi to the attention of international audiences. Eventually she was "discovered" by Mike Nichols, who staged her characters for the 1984-85 Broadway season. Furthering her fame, the show was filmed by HBO, where it has been shown often since it was first broadcast in 1985. Then came her screen debut as Celie in *The Color Purple*.

I won't bother to comment on *Purple* (page 35), except to state the obvious. After her first film, there was no doubt that this woman was a gifted actress. And since she had already proven herself as a club and theatrical comedienne, Hollywood dubbed her a hot property and eagerly set out to exploit the star potential of this brilliant comic/actress.

The trouble was that they had no idea what to *do* with her. Women comic actors of any description have it very rough in movieland. (Comedy has always been considered male turf.) But a funny BLACK woman? And *this* one in particular? For god's sake, the woman wears dreadlocks! If she had a long-legged perfect figure, classic (i.e., white) beauty, straightened hair, and a sultry (i.e., sexually exploitable) femininity, the studio execs would have known what to do. (It wouldn't have been pretty.) But, as she was?

Spielberg's extravaganza was no help in judging the possibilities. *Purple* was a period piece with an all-black cast, but what were they going to do with a Whoopi Goldberg in a contemporary story for a general release (read: white audience) movie? Ours is a film industry so short-sighted that it is unable to envision a black woman as anything other than a street prostitute or a maid. Whoopi must have, therefore, had them completely flummoxed. What kind of movie could they build around a small, androgynous black woman who defies characterization as a sex object or lackey?

Maybe it was beginner's luck, but they almost pulled it off in Whoopi's first comedy. *Jumpin' Jack Flash* is her best movie to date. It nonetheless clearly illustrates the problems involved. Whoopi's first comedy was also Penny Marshall's first feature directorial credit. Both of them did fine work here. It's the weak concept and mess of a screenplay by David H. Franzoni, J. W. Melville, Patricia Irving, and Christopher Thompson (It's always a bad sign when the writer credit reads like a cast list!) that almost scuttled the project.

The basic story concerns a bank computer operator, Terry Doolittle (Goldberg), with responsibilities for international transactions. She has a hacker's gift for computers and a born kibitzer's knack for making friends—even long distance via computer. She's gotten into trouble with her hard-ass boss about chitchatting with international colleagues on the company computer, but a reprimand from the boss is nothing compared to the trouble she finds on the other end of a knock-knock riddle that appears on her screen at closing time one night. A British intelligence agent is stranded behind the Iron Curtain, and Terry is apparently the only one who can help him get home.

Set aside, if you will, the issue of British spies and, to a lesser degree, CIA agents, being presented as good guys. It's a very real issue, but not unique to this movie. What is unique is Whoopi Goldberg's role as civilian hero in this comedy thriller. The good news is that Terry is shown to be (besides funny) intelligent, resourceful, brave, strong, honest, and caring. A girl scout, yes. But a humdinger of a girl scout.

Despite her virtue and heroism, she looks and acts much like women we know, or would *like* to know. Her wardrobe consists of baggy pants, tee shirts, baseball and Hawaiian shirts, and high-top sneaks. She keeps her Gumby and Pokey toys on her terminal at work, and her apartment is filled with old movie posters, toys, and books. Beyond the externals, she is a good friend to her co-workers and a *great* friend to Jack, the stranded agent. She's the kind of woman who'd go through hell, high water, or a paper shredder for a pal.

Terry can talk her way out of most fixes, but when that doesn't work, she has several tough-cookie self-defense techniques to call on that will have most guys in the audience yelping and covering their laps with the popcorn bucket. Her technological expertise, physical resourcefulness, and bravery are traits almost exclusively associated with male characters. As a matter of fact, Terry is one of the few adventure heroines I've ever seen who is given the same positive, no-nonsense attributes usually reserved for brave and intelligent men. As such, Terry, as Whoopi Goldberg brings her to life, is truly extraordinary.

Jumpin' Jack Flash allows Whoopi another unusual plus, the friendship of other women. Although we don't see much of them together, we see that Terry has several work friends, especially Carol Kane as a ditzy blonde with an active sex life who wants Terry to get out more. Terry is able to establish new friendships with women readily as well. Annie Potts plays a CIA wife who trusts and assists Terry as much as she can, even claiming her as a cousin. Since most Hollywood movies isolate women from one another, *Jack* gets relatively high marks in this area.

Sounds like a great movie. And it is, in portraying the hero as female. Whoopi is a positive image of a non-stereotypical woman who gets along well with other women. It is in the area of race that the movie breaks down. Look at Whoopi's world. Except for two black co-workers (a pregnant computer operator who goes on maternity leave midway through the movie and a gravelly voiced guard) and some street punks who want to rape her, Goldberg is stranded in a white world.

At times the movie exploits this distortion in what could be construed as a positive manner, as when Whoopi tries to convince a white cop to investigate a killing she witnessed and he insists on treating her like a strung-out hooker, or when she crashes a British Consulate party as a Diana Ross impersonator, or when she breaks into an Elizabeth Arden salon to convince Lady Sarah (a snooty ex-lover of Jack's) to do something to help him. In these three instances, the movie actually plays with the contrasts between Goldberg and the controlling white culture, pointing out (gently, of course) its racism. By lampooning racist stereotypes and the fanatical pursuit of youth and beauty by upper-class white women, the movie makes a few good points. However, Goldberg's racial isolation is, in itself, an act of bigotry.

It is white racial queasiness that motivated the movie's weak premise in the first place. To make Whoopi want to risk her life for her mysterious Jack, the screenwriters felt compelled to have her fall in love with him. (Lead characters are supposed to have a romance and, anyway, everyone knows women are ruled by their romantic yearnings rather than disinterested altruism.) They could have made Jack black, too, of course. But I doubt that the thought ever seriously crossed their minds. Hollywood has always resisted using more than one black in a lead role. This being so, the screenwriters faced a tricky situation. They wanted their black female lead to fall in love with a white male without offending any of the thousands anti-miscegenationists in their white audience. Their solution: Have the guy she falls for be represented by a CRT throughout the entire movie! Have them come face to face only in the last thirty seconds. No sexy kisses, just a chaste hug when they meet and go off to lunch. Fade to credits. Leave the rest, for thems that wants it, to the imagination.

It's a clever solution to an age-old Hollywood race problem (similar to putting Sidney Poitier together with blind women and nuns way back when), but it creates an even greater problem. How do you sustain dramatic action and viewer interest when many of the movie's big moments consist of a woman talking to a computer terminal. It is difficult for someone of even Whoopi Goldberg's brilliance to fascinate an audience by tapping away at a keypad for most of a movie. The amazing thing is that she pulls it off, with a little help from the voice of Jack (Jonathan Pryce), which is added to his screen messages after she hears it for the first time on his phone machine.

One scene, in particular, shows the skill of Goldberg's performance and Marshall's direction. In it, Terry finally gives Jack his escape contact, indicating to him that she was helped by Lady Sarah. It's a very emotional scene with a great little moral thrown in ("Maybe if you left it to the women," Terry replies, "you wouldn't be playing these stupid games!"). It's funny. It's dramatic. It's even romantic. And it's all one woman alone in an empty office with a computer screen!

The concept of *Burglar*, Whoopi's second comedy, while stronger, was bungled badly in the execution. Whoopi plays the title character in a truly bizarre adaptation of Lawrence Block's "Burglar" mystery novel series. In the novels, Bernie is a white male. So, okay, make Bernie (now short for Bernice) a black woman. Great. What about the other characters? In the books the support characters include Bernie's close buddy, Carolyn, a dog groomer—and a lesbian. Don't get your hopes up. If you think a major studio is going to let Whoopi Goldberg have a close friend who is a lesbian, you must be overdue for a reality tune-up. The movie had to fill its secret quota for straight, white males in lead roles, so Bernie's lesbian best friend, Carolyn, is changed to...that's right, a heterosexual white male. And he is played (believe it, or believe it not) by the king of the movie geeks, Bob Goldthwait.

Burglar has a few strong points, most of them are associated with Whoopi's performance as another strong resourceful woman. Our high-minded burglar ("I'm not gonna hit someone who doesn't have it coming") is forced to solve a murder while evading the police (who think she's their killer). But Whoopi's isolation in a white world is much more pronounced here. And in *Burglar* she is more isolated from women as well.

Again, the producers faced the sticky romance issue. Two minorities are one too many, so a black guy was out again. And they couldn't figure out a way to substitute a computer for a white guy, again. So they just avoid the whole idea until the last thirty seconds. Then they throw Whoopi into bodily contact with a white man in a way so ambiguous it can't offend the white populace. In the scene, Bernie jumps on an ex-cop named Ray (G. W. Bailey) and brings him to the ground, but it is unclear whether she is hitting him or hitting *on* him. One can only hope it's the former, since Ray is the slimebag who blackmailed her into her dangerous predicament in the first place. Early in the movie, he even had the audacity to call her a "pickaninny" to her face.

But maybe, in a warped way, that *is* a reason for her to want him as a lover. Ray, in calling her a pickaninny, is the only character who in any way recognizes her as an African-American. Insulting as he may be, at least he *sees* that part of her identity, which is something all the other characters seem too embarrassed to do.

The isolation of Whoopi in these movies is frightening. By refusing to deal with a black woman as a full, social human being, Hollywood instead treats their star like a pariah. Where is this woman's family? Her community? At times it seems that she is the only person of color in San Francisco or New York! They repeatedly deny her a racial identity. And by painting themselves into that particular corner, they are forced by their dread of miscegenation to deny her a sexual identity as well.

From the sound of the reviews, *Fatal Beauty* is worse. There was no mistaking the racism of the studio, MGM, this time. One of the myriad of reasons that the movie flopped was, again, that the film's "romance" made no sense. And it made no sense because a crucial scene was cut from the movie before the studio would release it. In *Fatal Beauty* Whoopi plays an undercover detective named Rita Rizzoli who is trying to track the source of some poisonous cocaine. For once, it almost looked like someone was going to give her a real, hot-kisses and such love interest. They wrote the script (originally intended, they say, for Cher) and shot it with a lover for Rita. The lover is—that's right—a white male. Well, almost.

Whoopi and Sam Elliot, who played the male lead, filmed a bedroom scene, but it never made it to the movie theaters. MGM forced the filmmakers, over the pleas and protests of both Goldberg and Elliot, to cut the scene from the film. All that's left is a "chaste" kiss in the released version, *again* occurring in the last thirty seconds.

Whoopi, who recognizes racism when she sees it, fought back the only way she could, through the press. She told *Jet* magazine: "If Sam Elliot had put some money on the table after the love-making scene, it would still have been in there." A strong statement, but undoubtedly true. Hollywood knows that white Americans are perfectly willing to watch a white master rape a black slave, or a white john use a black prostitute (both of which have been shown on screen many times before), but Hollywood isn't ready to show loving sexuality between equals of different races, especially if it is the woman who is black.

The fact that Whoopi Goldberg publicly charged MGM with the racism they and every other major studio practice constantly is important. It was a noble gesture, but probably a very foolish one if she wants to continue working in Hollywood. More recently, she actually sued New World Pictures and her director, Rip Torn, to block the release of her new movie, *The Telephone*. She had been promised a final cut approval which she didn't get. She took them to court, but lost her suit. But it looks like New World is stopping release on its own. At least for now. There's no happy ending to this one, either way.

Whoopi Goldberg's screen experiences are definitely going from bad to worse. The American film industry saw the star quality of this woman and was eager to exploit it and her, on their own terms. But by making her into an anomaly without a racial identity or sexuality, and without family or community, they are, perversely, forcing her to fail. And now that she has shown that she is not willing to accept that failure gracefully, now that she is calling them on their racism, she is also being labeled a troublemaker.

As an African-American woman seeking lead performances in motion pictures, Whoopi Goldberg faces an uphill battle. Anyone who has watched the careers of black male performers like Richard Pryor knows how difficult her struggle is. Pryor has the advantage of his manhood, at least, and look at the way Hollywood has squandered and demeaned (in unforgivable films like *The Toy*) his comic genius!

Then look at the career of, say, Robin Williams. He, too, is a unique and absolutely brilliant comic actor. Look at the quality and depth of the roles he has been given. Some are clunkers, sure. But most are not. In his movies, Williams is a man with a complete identity who is integrated fully into his social environment. Or, if he isn't (as in *Good Morning Vietnam*), it's because there is something wrong with his environment, not something wrong with *him*. Williams is a man in context. He is a man with a family, friends, someone to sleep with.

If only his friend Whoopi Goldberg could get the same treatment by Hollywood. Some critics content themselves to blame the victim—Goldberg—for the turkeys she has recently appeared in. They question her talent, or, at the very least, her judgment. But what choice does she really have? As bad as *Fatal Beauty* and *The Telephone* undoubtedly are, they were, in all likelihood, the best (least stereotypical) vehicles offered to her. As Robert Townsend trenchantly illustrated in *The Hollywood Shuffle*, the majority of parts for black actors still consist of slaves and servants, pimps and prostitutes, and dead-eyed junkies.

Whoopi Goldberg is brilliant and beautiful and a joy to watch. Hollywood knows it, and still they seem intent on ruining her. I could weep! It's such a stupid, bloody waste. But that's what racism is all about.

Hello Again

Not Nasty, Not Funny

To be funny without being hateful is practically impossible, at least to judge by American culture. Comedy is almost always based on physical pain and discomfort (the kick in the pants, the pratfall), or humiliation and mental cruelty (the pie in the face, the one-line "zinger" insult.) Much of it, over the years, is indicative of general misanthropy—and specific misogyny. For an example you need to go no further than the trailers, plastered all over the TV these days, for Danny DeVito's new film, *Throw Momma From the Train* ("I'll kill your wife. You kill my momma. That's fair!").

What? You don't find that hilarious? That's precisely why women, especially feminists, are accused of having "no sense of humor." Most of us are trying to get away from cruelty and pain in our own lives, and we want the same for others. For us, American comedy is usually an uncomfortable rather than an enjoyable experience.

I recently saw the first five minutes of a cable comedy special starring hot young comedian (and "St. Elsewhere" star) Howie Mandel. I saw only the first five minutes because I refused to stay in the same room with it any longer. His entire opening gambit consisted of making fun of Hawaiian culture and obesity. After a few stage yuks, he went into his audience, picked out several large women, and proceeded to insult them verbally and commit acts of humiliating physical schtick upon them. (And, of course, they were expected to be good sports about it all!)

Distressingly, traditional female comedians like Phyllis

Diller and Joan Rivers aren't much better. The only difference is that they exhibit as much hatred of themselves and their own bodies as they do of other women.

Many women (and humanistic menfolks) are now trying to find gentler forms of comedy based in shared human experience and a celebration of our differences. When it works, it's wonderful. That's why people get so high on Lily Tomlin/Jane Wagner routines, and the work of Whoopi Goldberg, and even Elayne Boosler's stand-up act. That's also why several radical feminists in my acquaintance would gladly postpone the revolution for a chance to see *Annie Hall* again.

The problem is that humanistic comedy is harder to pull off. It may not be mean. But it may not be funny either. A perfect example of a failed comedy with a heart of gold is Shelley Long's latest movie, *Hello Again*.

In the great tradition of sweet, screwball, back-from-the-beyond comedies like *Here Comes Mr. Jordan*, *Heaven Can Wait*, and *Topper*, *Hello Again* is the story of someone struck down in the prime of life, who returns to the land of the living once more. But this time, the resurrected hero is female. Lucy Chadman (Long) is a happy homemaker with a terminal case of clumsies. After a series of benign blunders and embarrassing mishaps, she chokes to death while nibbling a piece of her sister's South Korean chicken ball.

A handsome doctor tries to save her with nothing but a gentle word ("Come on, try for me!") and the power of his lovely blue-eyed gaze. He doesn't try CPR or use a cardioverter. It's a ludicrously passive approach for an emergency room physician to take. But while the male doctors in this movie are an inactive lot, Lucy's sister Zelda (Judith Ivey) is assuredly not. She not only mourns the passing of her sister, she wants to figure out a way to do something about it.

As proprietor of Cosmic Light Books in New York, she is a woman open to all the New Age arts. While going through books once owned by a "white witch in Sandusky," she discovers just the source she needs. *The Wisdom of Catagonia* informs her that it *is* possible to bring back one who dies before her time, given the right planetary configuration and timing, and provided that the lost one is a good soul and a ritual is performed exactly one year after the death by someone whose love for the deceased is "utterly pure." Zelda has the winning combination. To her joy, she is able to summon Lucy back to life with a rousing "Lucy, Goldo Win-jah!"

The world is not the same as Lucy left it, however. Her shallow and ambitious husband Jason (Corbin Bernsen) has already re-married, to Lucy's equally shallow and beauteous best friend, Kim (Sela Ward). They are living the high life in New York pushing Jason's career as plastic surgeon to high society, and going from posh party to posh party, as happy as pigs in mud. The last thing they want is a complication and embarrassment like Lucy, the homey klutz.

Zelda is certainly glad to have her sister back, and so is Lucy's grown and recently married son. The lovely blue-eyed doctor (Gabriel Byrne) is also interested in the new Lucy—and not *just* because she is a freak of science. Lucy has widening circle of support, even without her fickle husband. But life is still far too complicated for her. She is a one-of-a-kind displaced homemaker who must figure out what to do with the rest of her life. Which may not be a very long time. A footnote to Zelda's incantation informs her that her sister must find "true love" by the next full moon, or she will pass away again.

If you don't find that a particularly hilarious situation, you are not alone. Screenwriter and co-producer Susan Issacs has a hard time milking Lucy's second coming for laughs too. As for director Frank Perry, he is one of the most plodding and dull-witted directors in Hollywood today. He's just not meant for comedy—especially when the comedy demands a light touch.

When in doubt, which is often, Perry and Issacs have

Shelley Long trip on her own feet, or fall out of her dress, or get sauce down the front of her frilly blouse at a formal dinner party. The physical business becomes very predictable, yet never seems to jive with Lucy's personality. The dialogue shows even less imagination. Long is forced to say lines like "I wouldn't be caught dead in that dress" for laughs.

Dear, much maligned Shelley makes a valiant effort to rise above her lackluster lines and stiff direction. Her performance is sweeter and more open than any I've seen her give. And several of the support performances are equally endearing, like those of Thor Fields as Lucy's son and Austin Pendleton as a shy billionaire who falls in love with Zelda.

But there is far too little zaniness in *Hello Again*. There are no real belly laughs, and precious few chuckles. Still, there is a warmth to the movie that should not be dismissed as unimportant. Most of the characters in *Hello Again* are genuinely "nice." As for romantic happy endings (and subsequent bundles of joy), *Hello Again* has almost too many to count.

Precipitous couplings and baby-making aside, the key bond in this film is still that of Lucy and Zelda. They truly do have an "utterly pure" love for one another. Their relationship is one of total acceptance—Lucy of Zelda's "eccentricity" and Zelda of Lucy's two left feet. And there is something truly touching about Lucy's reunion with her son Danny. He has kept her herbs alive, and her favorite orange-crate art framed in his kitchen. And he has clearly kept her memory alive in his heart.

Hello Again has plenty of that rare commodity: heart. It also has a lovable woman hero and nary a mean bone in its celluloid body. So, unlike just about any other review you're likely to see, mine gives *Hello Again* the proverbial "thumbs up." Try not to expect hilarity. Try instead to remember that modern American hilarity is too often based on hurt and hate, elements mercifully absent from *Hello Again*.

Forgive its trespasses. This is, after all, a movie—from Hollywood—about a woman, brought back to life by the love of her sister, who gives new purpose to her new life by fighting for, and starting, a day-care center. There ain't a lot of humor, but what there is *good*-humored. Which makes *Hello Again* an amiable alternative to the likes of *Throw Momma From the Train*.

Dirty Dancing and Maid to Order

Made-to-Order Snobbery

The rich will always be with us. Especially on our movie screens. For every blue-collar character with a major role in an American movie, there has got to be a hundred upper-middle-class or out-and-out wealthy types. I guess we're all supposed to be fascinated with the way the other half (or, rather, the other fourth) live. I don't know how true the portraits of the rich are in American movies. But then, I don't much care. The rich can take care of themselves. And when they can't, they can hire someone else to do it. But I do care how working people are portrayed in the movies. And that's badly. A look at two current lightweight movies reminds me that even films that purport to satirize the rich and reinforce liberal values have some very warped ideas about class in America.

Dirty Dancing is the first production of Vestron Pictures, and it looks like they've started out with a mega-hit. It's a good, old-fashioned dance movie, complete with star-crossed lovers from different sides of the tracks. It is also a female coming-of-age movie about an idealistic young girl's first awakening, both to her sexuality and to the unfairness of life for the masses. Nothing heavy-duty, of course. Just a cheerful movie with a woman hero with it's heart, supposedly, in the right place.

Dirty Dancing is the brainchild of its co-producer and writer, Eleanor Bergstein, and it is said to be, in some measure, autobiographical. It tells the story of Baby Houseman (Jennifer Gray) during the summer of 1963. It is the summer before President Kennedy died, and the summer before Baby enters college at Mt. Holyoke. She is spending a vacation with her parents and sister at a Catskills resort called Kellerman's.

Baby, despite the diminutive nickname, is not a stereotyped Jewish American Princess. She *has* led a sheltered life, but dreams of helping others. She wants to study third-world economics at college and follow that with a stint in the Peace Corps. Her doctor-father (Jerry Orbach) is proud and indulgent of his favorite daughter's leftish leanings. "Our Baby's going to change the world!" he brags. And as much as she knows how to, Baby lives her ideals. She surprises a bellhop by helping to carry in her family's bags, and so endears herself to him that he breaks the class restrictions of the resort and lets Baby crash a staff party.

Class barriers are really what *Dirty Dancing*'s hole-ridden plot is about. The class structure at Kellerman's is plainly demarcated and rigidly enforced. The guests and management of the resort, all rich or upper-middle class, are at the top. Next come the "college boys" who are hired from Ivy League schools to work as waiters (you sure can tell this is twenty-five years ago!) in the dining room. These young fellows are encouraged, almost ordered, by the head man (Jack Weston) to "show the goddamn daughters a good time." They are, after all, the social equals of the guests. Not so the other help. The other employees (everyone from kitchen help to dance instructors) are considered hoi poloi. If *they* mix with the guests, they are subject to dismissal. It's that kind of class division that Baby wants no part of.

Like her lead character, Bergstein has tried to be impeccably liberal, but the condescension inherent in her attitude greatly diminished my enjoyment of her story. Let's start, for example, with the forbidden dance party that bellhop takes Baby to. Billy tries to talk Baby out of coming with him, but since he is having a hard time holding onto the watermelons (Yeah! You know dem po' folks love dat watermelon) he is carrying, he allows her to help. What Baby sees behind the doors of the rustic cabin leaves her thunderstruck.

In smoky, steamy close quarters, men and women of all races (and this is supposed to be 1963?) dance together in an energetic and exaggerated parody of sex. This is the "dirty dancing" of the title. And it's like nothing Baby has ever seen.

It's like nothing I've ever seen either! The choreography is so well done, and the dancing so sensuous and energetic, that as a member of the audience, it's hard not to be blown away, like Baby, by it. But I was made very uncomfortable by the way this party scene portrayed working people. The message seems to be that the laboring classes are primal savages who can work all day at their manual chores, and then do sweaty, sexy dances all night long, only stopping for a slice of watermelon.

Maybe I'm over-reacting here. But having come from a family that included a lot of hotel employees, I can tell you that in my family they started their shifts at 6:00 a.m. and didn't do much primal dancing late at night. They had a hot meal, a couple of drinks, and on a really rough day, a good foot soak in front of the TV. My version isn't very romantic or "dirty." Only more real.

Granted, no one said that *Dirty Dancing* was meant as social realism. But, in many ways, it puts on such a veneer with its pseudo-serious story line. As the plot develops, Baby falls under the spell of Johnny Castle (Patrick Swayze), who teaches dances like the merengue and the mambo to dowagers and their daughters. At the bottom of the Kellerman chain of being, Johnny keeps his emotional distance from the guests. He avoids the smitten Baby too, until she proves her benevolence by helping Johnny's best friend and professional dance partner, Penny (Cynthia Rhodes), who currently has big trouble.

Penny is pregnant by one of the Ivy League waiters. Baby's first attempts to be of help are rebuffed. "Go back to your playpen, Baby," Penny tells her. But Baby is genuinely concerned and does everything she can to help. She confronts the waiter and lashes out at his elitist contempt

("Some people count. Some people don't.") for his ex-lover. Robbie offers to lend Baby a copy of *The Fountainhead*, but refuses to help Penny with the cost of an illegal abortion.

Have no fear, Baby is here, to be Penny's personal savior. First she gets the abortion money (without admitting what it's for) from her father, and when Penny says she can't make her abortion appointment because she has to do a mambo demonstration at another hotel with Johnny, Baby offers to fill in as Johnny's partner. Then, when the abortion turns out to be a butcher job, Baby calls on Dad again for his medical assistance.

She's quite the well-intentioned little bee, our Baby. But it wouldn't make much of a movie if Baby didn't have her share of heartache, as well as humanitarian acts. And her heartache is Johnny. Dad, upset that Baby would have anything to do with something "illegal" (abortion) and then lie to him about it, has forbidden her from having anything more to do with "those people." Baby disobeys. In secret. She is in love with Johnny, and can't seem to leave her lowly stallion in his tight black pants alone.

The story line now reverts to standard star-crossed lovers gimmickry. Young love is almost torn asunder by various misunderstandings (e.g., the reason Baby's Dad is so down on Johnny) that could easily have been cleared up if any of the characters talked sensibly to one another. They don't. Although they do all make speeches. None of their proclamations of love and anger sound like natural conversations but some of them are effective nonetheless. When Baby confesses to the lies she told her father, she adds, "But you lied, too. You told me everyone's alike and deserved a fair shake. But you meant everyone who was like you."

In scenes like that one, Bergstein seems to be sincerely critical of upper-middle-class liberalism, but she falls into some of the same pitfalls she wants to criticize. Bergstein's people aren't any more "alike" than Dr. Houseman's. Her upper-class characters are the movie's movers and shakers. The only thing the poor seem to be able to do for themselves is dance. Johnny and Penny, both of who are older than Baby and survivors of a rough childhood, are oddly helpless. Without the championship of Baby, you get the feeling they never would have solved their problems. Couldn't Johnny have collected the needed abortion money among his dirty dancing playmates? Couldn't another of those hot female dancers (who, at least, already *know* the mambo—unlike our heroine) have filled in for Penny at the exhibition performance? Evidently not. Baby is the only one who can save the day.

The passivity of the working class characters is compounded in *Dirty Dancing* by their self-hatred. Johnny seems to agree with the neo-Nazi in the waiter's jacket about his lack of worth. Johnny says, "The reason people treat me like nothing is that I *am* nothing." A stupid and unbelievable line, eerily similar to Robbie's statement that some people matter and some don't!

Baby never wonders if she's "nothing" and that's good to see in a central female character. It's also nice to see the female hero as the character who changes everyone's life for the better. It feels good to see her triumph at the movie's end, universally loved and admired. And Jennifer Gray as Baby portrays the character as a genuinely good and caring (but not too nice-nice) girl. How can you think badly of her? In fact, I can't fault Gray's performance, or that of Swayze or Rhodes. They do what they can with their lines and create very sympathetic characters with them.

The problem is with Bergstein's script. It is filled with cliches and false class assumptions from the start to the hokey ending. In the final scene, Johnny crashes the end-of-season party to perform his dance routine and to publicly thank Baby for deigning to care for his plebian self. He tells the assembled crowd that Baby, now called Frances, is "somebody who's taught me about the kind of person I want to be." It's an embarrassing speech, especially when it isn't followed by a companion speech of thanks from Baby. Baby never thanks Johnny for his love, or for challenging her to stand up to her father, or for teaching her about living her politics. She doesn't thank him at all. She just beams and dances, the deserving little Princess.

It's ironic, really, that a movie which hopes to censure phony liberalism is so filled with it. The intelligent, active, heroic character is from a privileged background and retains her privilege. The under-privileged characters are naive, self-hating, and unable to help themselves. They are sexual and can dance to a jungle rhythm, but are dependent on and pathetically grateful for the championship of their social betters.

Oh well. What can you expect from a dance movie? At least the dancing *is* very good. Amy Jones's new movie doesn't even have that much going for it. It does have the dynamite singing of Merry Clayton. But, of course, the movie isn't *about* a black woman who can sing. *Maid to Order* is about the lessons learned by another daughter of privilege. This time, she is filthy rich. Her name is Jessie Montgomery, and she is played by second-generation feminist Ally Sheedy.

Jessie is an aimless user of the upper class. She sleeps all day and parties all night. Her biggest sin seems to be that she spends too much of the unearned cash of her widowed father (Tom Skerritt). His idle wish on a star that he "never had a daughter" comes true. And Jessie, arrested for speeding, DWI, and cocaine possession, finds that her father no longer knows who she is. Without his money and influence, who's going to get her out of her scrapes?

A fairy godmother, played by Beverly D'Angelo, that's who. Although D'Angelo's Stella sure isn't my idea of a nurturing fairy godmother. Except for springing Jessie from jail, Stella seems more punishing than supportive. D'Angelo is, for all intents, a mere plot device. She appears on the scene to deliver threats to Jessie that she'll never get her life back unless she straightens up. She abandons Jessie with no friends or family, and only a pocketful of loose change, in a city park. "Get a job. Then we'll talk."

Nine years in junior college have left Jessie trained for

nothing, so she wanders into a domestic placement agency and is greeted with joyous welcome. Seems that "there's no such thing as a white maid in Los Angeles," so Jessie is embraced as the Great White Hope. The agency places her the same day in the home of a nouveau riche couple played for broad farce by Dick Shawn and Valerie Perrine.

Here's where class nastiness actually causes a stylistic problem for the movie. While the other characters are played straight, Shawn and Perrine, as Stan and Georgette Starkey, are played as absolute buffoons. Perrine, who dresses like a Frederick's of Hollywood bimbo, is an obsessive tight-wad. She hoards old newspaper to sell and screams at her cook, Audrey (Merry Clayton), for throwing away a four-inch square of used aluminum foil.

Why does it seem that Shawn and Perrine are in a different movie than the rest of the cast? I think it has to do with who it is acceptable to make fun of in this country. Jones and co-screenwriters, Perry and Randy Howze, must have known that it is no longer cool to make fun of black and Hispanic servants in too obvious a manner, so they had to find another butt for their miserable humor. A white, nouveau riche couple is perfect. Their loud, gum-chewing egotism and their equally loud wardrobe finger them as upwardly mobile working class yokels who've gotten above themselves.

Compare the Starkeys to characters representing *old* wealth. Jessie's father, Charles Montgomery, is portrayed as a quiet, caring, perfect gentleman, who likes nothing better than to share his wealth with the less fortunate. He's even polite to the Starkeys, although he clearly sees them as grasping peasants with no taste or refinement.

And as for Jessie, she is a rich girl who needs to be knocked down a peg or two, but only so she'll be more responsible with her father's millions and kinder to servants. As Jessie is initially played, she certainly deserves a few knocks, but placing her with the Starkeys is a cheap trick. Think about the same situation if this bratty girl had to learn her lesson by being placed in her own father's household where she could really see how different "downstairs" feels from "upstairs." Now *that* might be interesting.

The entire humiliate-the-rich-girl concept of *Maid to Order* is, I think, a bad idea in more ways than one. It is hard to hang a movie on a character as unsympathetic as Jessie. And, after all, this is a rich character whom we feel sure will get back to her heiress status by the end of the movie. So you still have a privileged hero.

Earlier classic servant comedies like *My Man Godfrey* (1936) had a more humanistic intent. In *Godfrey*, William Powell plays a hobo adopted by Carole Lombard to be her wacky rich family's new servant. It is the poor servant who teaches his rich employers about maturity, respect, and caring for other people. You eventually learn that Godfrey, too, is a former member of the upper crust, but any humbling he had coming occurs before the action of the movie starts. He is heroic from the very beginning.

More recently, a somewhat similar film, *Down and Out in Beverly Hills* (1986), presented a male hobo, played by Nick Nolte, who changed for the better the messed-up selfish lives of an affluent California clan.

Godfrey and *Down and Out* may not be any more believable than *Maid to Order*, but they are, at least, easier to accept from a class standpoint. The sexual politics of the three films is something else worth pondering. Unlike the two male movies in which the hero is a swell guy from the start, *Maid to Order* sets up Jessie as a rich bitch and then invites us to enjoy her humbling and humiliation. I can't help wondering if the film would have been made the same way with the man as the humbled hero.

Like *Dirty Dancing*, the folks behind *Maid to Order* thought, I'm sure, that they were making a terribly liberal movie. But showing a rich man of inherited wealth as a saintly philanthropist and working class people who make it as gauche and self-centered oafs doesn't look very forward-thinking to me. Watching two hours of an unsympathetic female hero being humiliated until she learns to be a good girl who knows how to cook and clean a house doesn't go over big with me either.

Merry Clayton, a promising actress and dynamite singer (remember the back-up vocal for "Gimme Shelter" that so showed up the "blue-eyed" soul of Mick Jagger? Remember Sisters Love?), is wonderful in *Maid to Order*, but absolutely wasted. I'd like to see her as the central figure in a movie. Not as a maid or a cook, either. I wish Ally Sheedy better luck next time, too.

Dirty Dancing and *Maid to Order* are meant as light entertainment with positive messages about social equality in the U.S. The light entertainment is there, especially in the exuberant dance of *Dirty Dancing*. The message is there, too. But it's not a positive one. Both movies prove that we are not created equal. Heroic and active figures in life have money. As for the working joes, if they're lucky they'll be sponsored toward a better life by a rich benefactor. But they shouldn't get too lucky. If they try to crash the gentry, their total lack of taste and refinement will give them away, and like the Starkeys, they'll only make fools of themselves.

That was our class lesson for today from the guys and gals who make the movies.

Women Make Movies

Desert Hearts

Donna Deitch's Big Gamble

The most amazing thing about the film *Desert Hearts* is that it was ever made at all. And it *wouldn't* have been made without the total dedication of the movie's producer and director, Donna Deitch. Deitch faced the challenges all women directors face when they try to make the leap from documentaries (hers include *The Great Wall of Los Angeles* and *Woman to Woman*) into feature film. She also faced a unique (some would have thought insurmountable) challenge that other American women directors have *not* faced. Deitch wanted her first feature film to be a love story between two women.

When Donna Deitch first read Jane Rule's novel *Desert of the Heart*, she was drawn to the love story and to the "central metaphor" of the story: people gambling their money away in the casinos of Reno, while others, particularly the two female leads, gamble with their sexuality and social identity as they defy taboos to find true love.

You can see why Deitch was so drawn to a story about risk-takers, since she is a big-time risk-taker herself. After falling in love with the novel, she coaxed the movie rights from Rule. She then spent two and a half years of her life raising the $1.5 million (peanuts in the world of feature film-making for a period movie) to finance the project. She wrote or phoned or met with everyone she ever knew—or heard of—who *might* have money to invest. She even sold her house to finance her dream. The gamble paid off, for her, and for us.

The film opens as a train pulls in to Reno. The time is 1959, and Vivian Bell (Helen Shaver), an English professor from Columbia, has come west to get a divorce. She takes up residence at the dude ranch of Frances Parker (Audra Lindley), and wants nothing more than to hide away with her books. But while she can avoid the other divorcees and spend a minimum of time with Frances and her fresh-faced son, Walter (Alex McArthur), she can't seem to stay away from Cay Rivvers, Walter's half-sister.

Cay (Patricia Charbonneau) is a lanky, casual young woman with a direct gaze and a kind of horsey beauty. The first time Vivian sees Cay is as Frances drives her, for the first time, to the ranch. Driving in the opposite direction on her way to Reno, Cay stops to say hello by driving next to Frances' station wagon, doing 60 mph—in reverse! A dashing risk-taker in sexual matters, too, Cay makes it no secret that she is a lesbian. She is confident in and comfortable with her sexuality, and expects the same of those around her.

Vivian *isn't* comfortable with Cay's sexuality. But she's not comfortable with her own sexuality either. "You drown in still waters," she tells Cay when asked the reason for her divorce. Shaver's Vivian is so tense and inhibited that she, at times, appears wooden. This is no criticism of Helen Shaver's sensitive performance. Shaver's guarded expression and stiff carriage are absolutely right in a woman just starting to surface after years of emotional and sexual suppression.

Sharing the front seat with Cay and one of her casual female lovers, Vivian is comically stuffy. Later in their friendship, Cay kisses her through an open car window, and we see Vivian's hands clenched in her lap, and there is nothing funny about her terror. Vivian wants "to be free of who [she's] been." And she wants Cay. But that doesn't keep her from panicking every time Cay gets too close. Vivian is terrified of letting go. She's also frightened of crossing the line from married, heterosexual respectability, to the great unknown of being a lesbian in a straight world.

Vivian's awkwardness and fear are one of the things I liked best about Natalie Cooper's screenplay and Deitch's direction in comparison to Rule's novel. Rule imbued her "Vivian" with a surprising lack of resistance to her lesbian awakening. It makes a nice fantasy, but always seemed unbelievable to me. It seems more likely that a woman who has identified herself as straight for all her life, especially given the buttoned-down year of 1959, would indeed vacillate mightily before gathering the courage to take another woman as her lover.

In Deitch's and Cooper's version of the story, Cay has to practically throw herself at the timid professor. It takes a little bare-breasted persuasion, but when Vivian's resistance gives way, it is in one of the sexiest mutual seductions to ever hit the screen. We're talking steamy here. When Vivian and Cay make love, the earth moves in ways that rival the Nevada nuclear test explosions.

Deitch's love scene is remarkable because it is honest and erotic. Something well-intentioned movies like *Lianna* and *By Design* (and less well-intentioned films like *Personal Best*) never achieved. Such movies seemed to accept the right of women to love one another but were coy, or downright embarrassed, about showing actual lovemaking between women. Since these films were directed by men, this is not surprising. You can imagine how broad-minded these fellows felt for making their lesbian leads nice, attractive people, all the while retaining their touching faith that you can't have real sex without a pecker.

Deitch gives us real sex, deeply passionate and affirming. And if it is somewhat unrealistic (our two lovers achieve simultaneous orgasm in their first encounter), it is certainly no more unrealistic than ninety percent of the heterosexual seductions Hollywood has given us over the years.

If Cooper's screenplay is at all coy, it is in the explication of the relationship of Cay and her casino co-worker, Silver (Andra Akers). Rule's novel makes it very clear that Silver and Cay are lovers, the movie is ambiguous on that score, as it is in disclosing the full extent of Cay's attempt to maintain a heterosexual relationship with her casino supervisor, Darell (Dean Butler). Whether these changes were caused by the streamlined needs of the screen, or by the filmmakers' fears that too many lovers would make Cay appear wanton, is something only Deitch and Cooper can answer.

A change that could have happened, but mercifully didn't, is the villainizing of men in the story. Deitch's men aren't monsters—if anything, they're even more affable than the men of the novel—they are merely immaterial to the story's major actions and emotions. Cay's half-brother Walter, who himself has a crush on Vivian, is a sweet young man. He teases his sister about success with women ("How you get all that traffic with no equipment is beyond me!"), but he accepts her unconditionally and supports her relationship with Vivian Bell. Silver's fiancé, Joe (Anthony Ponzini), is likewise a good guy. He even cooks dinner while Silver and Cay take a bubble bath together!

Deitch doesn't create a world completely without homophobia; Cay's male suitor, as well as her stepmother Frances, are angry and frightened by Cay's love for Vivian. But in each case, jealousy, and a gut fear of losing Cay, are the real operative emotions, and not a hatred of lesbianism.

It's unlikely that this failure to dwell on homophobic bigotry is accidental, either. By making it clear, through character interaction and the approbation of her camera, that Cay's and Vivian's relationship is inevitable and right, Deitch demands the same approval from her audience. By teaching through example, Deitch is able to instruct without browbeating, and without seeming to proslytize at all.

In this way, a simple, old-fashioned, and very romantic love story becomes a very political piece of work. In the natural way Deitch handles a subject viewed by many as unnatural, in her cheerful determination to show things the way they ought to have been instead of the way they too often were, and are, she challenges her straight audience to be just as accepting, and validates and celebrates the lives of her gay audience.

This is, of course, no small achievement. The fact that Deitch pulls it off so well proves that *Desert Hearts* is a film of great importance, regardless of the occasional awkwardness of the script and infrequent technical clumsiness (e.g., cumbersome "wipe" scene transitions). No doubt such problems stem from the bare bones budgeting and tight shooting schedule of *Desert Hearts*. It makes you wonder what Donna Deitch could do with a standard Hollywood budget. Let's hope we get to find out some day very soon.

Desert Hearts is not a movie everyone will love. Except for the sex scene (during which *everyone* sits up and takes notice), the film is often slow-moving. There are those who will even find it dull. I'm not one of them. On the contrary, I think Deitch is to be congratulated for refusing to sensationalize her material. The actors, none of whom had high name recognition, are also to be commended for their fine, controlled performances. Worthy of special mention are Patricia Charbonneau as Cay and Audra Lindley as Frances.

A friend's experience seeing *Desert Hearts* soon after it opened in New York says it all. She had escaped from an oppressive weekend visit with her family to see the movie and had been energized and elated by it. Afterwards, in the theater's restroom, she listened to the embarrassed protestations of a woman who was outraged by the film's content and felt the need (surely the lady protested too much!) to assure the women around her that she didn't understand why such a movie was ever made, that it didn't interest her in the least.

"Well, it interests *me*," my friend informed her. "It's important to *me*."

Desert Hearts is important to so many of us. And yet, I'd like to think that, in the long run, it will turn out to be even more important (as an eye-opening, consciousness-raising experience) to hostile witnesses like that woman in the restroom, people who might see the film by accident in a theater, or on tape or cable, and in some way be touched by it. *That* would be the biggest and best payoff Donna Deitch could receive from her grand, first, feature film gamble.

Desperately Seeking Susan

Worth Seeking Out

"Desperate...I *love* that word," sighs Roberta Glass (Rosanna Arquette), *Desperately Seeking Susan*'s heroine, as she moons over the personals in a New York tabloid. A man named Jim (Robert Joy) is once again "desperately seeking Susan," his inconstant lover. The two stay in touch via the personals, and Roberta stays in touch with her romantic fantasies by following the exploits of Susan (Madonna) as she flits from city to city and man to man, with rock band leader Jim always keeping the home fires stoked.

Roberta's life as a Fort Lee, New Jersey, homemaker is stable and comfortable, but it lacks the romantic intensity of those who live and love on the wild side. So after her birthday party (a dismal affair where she hands around canapes to close personal friends like her husband's dentist and obediently watches with her guests as hubby shows off a new commercial for his "tub and spa" emporium), Roberta plots a vicarious thrill for herself. She will eavesdrop on the next reunion of Susan and her musician lover, the time and place having been noted in Jim's last ad.

The reunion proves a short one, but the mesmerized Roberta continues her clumsy tail on Susan. When she loses her quarry, Roberta comforts herself by buying her mercenary idol's sequined jacket (appropriately embroidered with the pyramid found on a dollar bill), which Susan has traded in an East Village boutique for glittery boots. She then rushes back to her fully programmed kitchen in Fort Lee.

The life of a voyeuristic innocent can, we soon learn, get mighty complicated. When Roberta places her own personal

Roberta Glass (Rosanna Arquette) in Desperately Seeking Susan.

in an attempt to find Susan again, she misses her punk heroine and instead finds herself, in her new jacket and pathetic attempt at new wave costuming, mistaken for Susan by bad guy and good guy alike. It seems that Susan's last lover, an Atlantic City hood, has been murdered by a gangster who thinks Susan now has the valuables for which he killed his cohort. It is only the appearance of Jim's friend Dez (Aidan Quinn), assigned to look after a woman he's never seen, that stops the gangster in mid-assault on Roberta— and she still gets a bop on the head that knocks her out and produces total amnesia. She awakens to find Dez calling her Susan and asking why the guy was hassling her. Roberta has no idea; all she has is a scrap of paper with Dez's phone number on it and a key to a Port Authority locker, evidence enough for the two of them that she is Susan. Against his better judgment, Dez takes the dazed "Susan" under his wing.

Dez is a reluctant knight, to be sure. Just dumped by his latest lover, he wants nothing more than to be left alone with his cat, his fish, and his B-movie collection. From what he's heard of Susan, she's definitely trouble, and he expects a manipulative woman who'll somehow do a number on him. What he finds is a sweet-natured, doe-eyed woman for whom "I'm sorry" is the basic conversational response. She's trouble, too. But he can't help but come to her repeated aid.

While Roberta and Dez rush through New York attempting to elude the ever-watchful gangster, the real Susan teams up with Roberta's uptight, would-be swinger of a husband in the wilds of Jersey. At this point the screwball tempo of director Susan Seidelman's comedy really picks up, with genuinely amusing if not wildly hilarious results.

In the midst of all the silliness and suspense, Roberta finds herself by losing her safe, agreeable, goody-goody self—and orgasmic sex with a nice man is only part of the process. There is a wellspring of strength and resourcefulness in Roberta. We see her joy and wonder as she earns her first twenty dollars as a magician's assistant, her dignity when she is busted as a prostitute. Being Susan frees her up, but not to become just another hip hedonist. Being Susan frees the real Roberta. When finally leaving a police holding tank (thanks to Dez's bail), Roberta assures the prostitute next to her that it was a pleasure meeting her. We are glad to know that Roberta will always be a nice girl from Jersey—as well as a woman with moxie and a growing sense of her own worth.

Seidelman's direction is assured, light-handed, and mercifully restrained in the shtick department: Leora Barish's script also avoids cheap laughs in favor of a certain absurd believability. As for the performances, there is nary a false move in a cast of little-known actors. Aidan Quinn, with his wiry body and soulful blue eyes, is especially appealing as the romantic interest. Dez wants to toughen up and be a user, but he just can't seem to manage it. The subtlety of Quinn's performance makes Dez very sympathetic—and very seductive.

Noteworthy among the supporting cast are Anna Levine as Susan's long-suffering woman friend, Mark Blum as Roberta's jerky spouse, and Laurie Metcalf as his sister, a woman who continues to search for a good man despite her gut belief that there aren't any. After cross-examining her brother about Roberta's sex life prior to her disappearance, she concludes that Gary Glass deserved to be left.

Madonna is, of course, the most famous member of the cast. She is the current queen of rock (her hits include "Like a Virgin," "Crazy for You," and "Material Girl"). The grasping, punkish, sex-kitten routine that Madonna does so well has always left me uneasy; its apparent satire is taken seriously by too many fans and detractors, and her role in *Desperately Seeking Susan* is very close to her musical persona. Susan is not someone I'd want any women to emulate, especially not our teenaged daughters.

Thanks to Seidelman, it is Roberta who remains the central figure and heroine to the film. And Rosanna Arquette couldn't be better as the vulnerable heroine who gets a crash course in street smarts and self-reliance. After Roberta's bewildering journey of self-discovery and her brave defense of the real Susan in the movie's frightening, farcical climax, we applaud (literally, at the showing I attended) the rewards she reaps, including a continuing romance with a nice, cat-and home-loving guy from New York.

Desperately Seeking Susan is a movie worth seeking out. It is funny, warm, and well-crafted. And, unlike the majority of Hollywood sex comedies, it leaves no bitter aftertaste.

Satisfaction

Up(?) from Exploitation

"Exploitation" is an oft used buzz-word in human and animal rights movements. In such circles, exploitation is, without doubt, a negative word. It's the enemy. It's what we want to end. The film industry also claims "exploitation" as a buzz-word. But, in movieland, exploitation is not a bad thing. It's the stock and trade. It's what you create to keep the customer satisfied. It is one of the grand (squalid, yet very profitable) traditions of the film biz.

Hard-core exploitation films have been around since the beginning of moving pictures. They are the underside of censored Hollywood, and they originally played at sideshows, burlesque houses, and "art" movie theaters. Exploitation flicks paraded all that was considered sinful and shocking before eager eyes. Everything a Hollywood, under the Motion Picture Production Code could only imply, exploitation films reveled in. T & A/B & G (tits and ass, blood and guts) were essential components of movies made cheaply and quickly for the enjoyment of a largely male audience. One could certainly argue that such films were and are pornography. Yet, since exploitation films are not usually just an episodic string of graphic sexual acts (in fact, sexual matters usually take a backseat to gore and other gross-outs), they are *generally* considered a separate category, falling on the sleazo-celluloid spectrum somewhere between porno and feature movie.

As the term exploitation implies, degradation is still a large part of their appeal. And the degradation of women, in particular, is often an intrinsic element. But as movie censorship loosened up, exploitation films changed. First they moved from the side show to the drive-in where they became the kind of movie Joe Bob Briggs (Movie Channel VJ) loves to rhapsodize about. Then as graphic violence became more acceptable; as sex, drugs, and rock 'n roll went up-scale; exploitation movie-making joined the mainstream.

What was once filmed in grainy black and white, burst into technicolor. With bigger budgets, production values rose. Slowly but surely, exploitation went Hollywood, where its influence is now felt in the majority of sex comedies and adventure films geared toward the younger (still male) crowd. Even low-budget schlockers have found a playground more lucrative than the drive-ins: the home video market. The American family, judging from my neighborhood video store, eats this stuff up. Or, to be more precise, they love to *watch* it while they *eat* their microwavable entrees.

Why this lengthy discourse on exploitation films? Because it is, sad to say, one of the main training grounds for the American woman director. It is mighty hard for anyone, especially a woman, to break into the directing field. Most of the handful of women directing feature films today broke in through the back door, making documentaries or low-budget exploitation flicks. Joan Freeman, director of the current teen movie, *Satisfaction*, is a good example. She did both.

Freeman graduated from Harvard in 1976 and entered the TV documentary field. She contributed segments to respected shows like PBS's *Nova*. Then, in 1985, with backing from one of the kings of the exploitation game, Roger Corman (creator of classics like *Swamp Woman* and *Bloody Mama*), she co-wrote and directed her first feature-length film, *Streetwalkin'*.

Streetwalkin' is, as you might imagine, a film about female prostitution. It no longer plays in movie houses, but can be seen, from time to time, on late-night cable. And it is currently available on videotape in a box illustrated with a young woman in hot pants with a come-hither stare.

"Take a rock-hard walk on the wild side with *Streetwalkin'!*"
advises the box. Now I know that you can't judge a tape by
its cover, but in some cases, the packaging fits the product.
If you think Freeman's film is going to be another *Working
Girls* (page 154), think again.

Streetwalkin' is the story of Cookie (Melissa Leo), a
teenaged woman who, along with her younger brother, is
driven from her home by a sexually abusive stepfather and
an alcoholic mother who takes his side. She's at the Port
Authority only a few minutes when she is approached by a
seemingly kindhearted gent named Duke. By the next scene,
Cookie is a Times Square hooker, living with Duke, her pimp.
Freeman doesn't show us this transformation. She gives us
no indication of what it was like for Cookie when she started
to work the streets. One minute, she's a scared kid. The next,
she's a street-smart prostitute.

Like Stephanie Rothman, a Corman-sponsored woman
director (of films like *The Student Nurses*, 1970) before her,
Freeman wanted, I think, to create a thoughtful movie, a slice
of urban verité. But, first and foremost, she had to serve the
demands of the exploitation market paying the bills. Meeting
the requirements of the exploitation formula without being
exploitative toward women is an impossible challenge, and
Joan Freeman is no Wonder Woman.

While most of Freeman's women *are* survivors, resourceful and sometimes supportive of one another, they (even
Cookie, the presumed heroine of the piece) are secondary
props to, and easy targets for, the orgy of male violence
acted out by Duke and his rival pimps.

The character of Duke has more in common with the
horror monsters of slasher movies than with men in realistic
drama. He beats and kicks his women, to death in one case,
and would like to do the same to most men he meets. His
general code of conduct is to brutalize or kill anyone who
tries to thwart him. Even three armed goons are no match
for him. By the end of the movie, the invincible Duke has
been punched, bludgeoned, shot, and run over by a car, but

he still has enough energy left to try to knife Cookie.

Assuming that you have the stomach to watch to the final frame, you will see that it is Cookie, her young brother, and an older earth-mother prostitute called Queen Bee who *finally* destroy Duke. The last scene is of our trio, embraced together, staggering away from Duke's bloody corpse toward the New York sunrise. It might have been an hopeful ending, except that by that point you are so stunned by all the violence that you are past caring about the triumph of the women and children over the male monster.

Queen Bee, a willowy Amazon in a red teddy and garter belt played by Julie Newmar (remember Catwoman on TV's *Batman* show?), is a real kick. And Leo's Bambi-with-a-backbone portrayal of Cookie shows real possibilities. The problem is that far too much of the film is taken up in orchestrated violence and sexual teasing. There's no time in the exploitation formula for extraneous matters like character development or emotional shading. We learn so little about these women, about what they think and feel, that it is hard to think or feel anything about them. The gritty pseudo-realism, shot at a distance, in the shadows, puts us off rather than draws us in. By failing to engage the audience's emotions, Joan Freeman's *Streetwalkin'* becomes just another exercise in rage and cruelty for those who are entertained by such things.

Freeman's new film brings her out of the back alleys and onto the beach in *Satisfaction*. A bigger budget, better-known cast, and sunnier locale make for a more cheerful and polished film, but Joan Freeman still hasn't figured out how to draw her audience into her story or characters. In this failure, she had help.

The screenplay, by Charles Purpura, is dull and cliche-ridden. As in far too many teen pictures, it is an insult to its audience. You can almost hear Aaron Spelling (co-producer and king of schlock TV) giving Purpura his assignment: Write a story about a bunch of girls graduating from high school. They're into rock and roll. They have a garage band. You know, something like The Bangles. They want one last summer of fun before knuckling down to their dull lives, so they go out to a ritzy beach resort where they play in a beach bar. Throw in the standard stuff—romance, heartbreak, drugs, rock music. It'll be great.

Great isn't the word. Boring is. Without the bloody violence and bare breasts of the exploitation formula, Freeman doesn't seem to know what to do to entertain her audience. Besides Freeman's phlegmatic direction, and Purpura's banal script, *Satisfaction* has a heavy burden to bear in its star, Justine Bateman. I *like* Justine Bateman. But one-dimensional bubbleheads (as she has played for several years on TV's "Family Ties") may be all she is capable of. Ms. Bateman appears to have little range—vocal or emotional. She should *never*, as she does here, sing. And as for her acting, she should choose her projects carefully, since she is one of the scores of attractive Hollywood ingenues who are only as good as their direction and material. Which means we're batting 0 for 3.

Satisfaction isn't a total disaster. A story about a group of women who are caring buddies always has its moments. And the rest of the cast, with the exception of Bateman's romantic interest, played by Liam Neeson, far outshine the star. Worthy of special praise are Trini Alvarado as the hoodiest of the girls and Scott Coffey as the shy, classically trained keyboardist who becomes the band's one male member.

The fact that Alvarado and Coffey can keep their embarrassment to themselves and almost have us believing this stunted story line is proof of their talent, but it isn't enough to recommend *Satisfaction*. For those who want a rock and roll movie with a little bite, I'd suggest renting Paul Schrader's *Light of Day*, which stars Justine's TV brother, Michael J. Fox, and Joan Jett. Jett's performance, both as a singer and an actor, is dynamite, and makes the maudlin excesses of the script more than bearable.

And if you feel the need to chase away those end-of-winter blues with a good beach picture, I recommend to you the work of another woman director, Lyndall Hobbs. *Back to the Beach*, the return of Annette Funicello and Frankie Avalon to the site of their beach blanket youth, is also at video stores. The music is good, and the pace is snappy. Best of all, this is a silly film that never tries to take itself seriously. The self-satire of *Back to the Beach* allows the audience to say "Boy, what a dumb, corny movie!" and still love every second of it. Joan Freeman should take a lesson.

The director of *Satisfaction* learned too many of her lessons in the dispassionate idiom of the documentary and the empty, bloody pyrotechnics of the exploitation film. Maybe she needs to do some un-learning of bad habits. Joan Freeman is not untalented. But until she learns to respect herself and her audience more, she'll probably never make a movie worth watching.

Bright Lights, Big City and High Tide

The Ways a Woman Can Be

It seems as though every time I exit a movie theater, I take my leave with a troubled mind and a puzzled expression. It's as though the final frame reads "What's wrong with this picture?" And I, the poor bewildered feminist viewer, have to somehow re-examine the film to figure out, for the sake of my own sanity, exactly what was screwy and mixed-up in what I just saw. Usually I lose count somewhere around item number thirty-five.

Macho flicks, in which women don't exist at all, are beginning to look more attractive than general films which show us stripped down (too often, literally) to the lowest common stereotype. I keep thinking things are going to change, but I begin to wonder whether it will be in my lifetime.

Recently I went to see *Bright Lights, Big City*, starring the adorable Michael J. Fox as a yuppie suffering from writer's block and cocaine addiction. His downspin is precipitated by the death, a year earlier, of his beloved mother and a more recent rejection by his fashion model wife. Abandoned by the two women he loves, any sensitive fellow will turn into a self-destructive jerk.

The portrayal of women in *Bright Lights, Big City* is a textbook travesty. Phoebe Cates, who plays the estranged wife, is listed third in the credits, directly behind Fox and Kiefer Sutherland, who plays (superbly, I might add) Fox's even more debauched best buddy. You might expect any woman listed high in the title credits to have a sizable part in a movie, but unless I fell asleep somewhere in the middle (which *is* possible, since watching a sweet puppy of a boy-man snort coke and guzzle alcohol for two hours has limited entertainment value for me), I'd swear that Cates had only three lines in the entire film.

She says hello to Fox twice, and in her big movie moment follows up one of her "Hi"s with a "How's it going?" *This* is the female lead of the movie?! Cates *looks* beautiful and unattainable, which is exactly what—and all—director James Bridges wanted of her, but we know nothing about who this woman is, and what *her* life is like.

In the most meaningful scene between the husband and wife, Fox talks to a *mannequin*, whose face was based on a life mask of his wife. He communes with the plaster effigy through a department store window. We get the point, boys. Amanda is a beautiful thing and airhead devoid of any real feelings, who can only cause suffering to the fragile male heart. Makes you wonder why they bothered to cast the part at all. Giving the female lead to the mannequin would have been just as effective and would have saved the producers a nice piece of change. (But I'm forgetting, that's already been done, more or less, in *Mannequin*, a film Kim Cattrall will *never* live down.)

The woman listed second in the ads for *Bright Lights* is Dianne Wiest, who plays the dead mother. She has a couple of well-acted deathbed scenes. (In one she finds her dying agony almost welcome, since it is a vivid reminder of labor pain and the intense love she bears her son.) Then, near the end of the movie, when the collapsing Jamie has finally reached his nadir, a healing image of his mother comes to him. She is smiling. She is standing in the kitchen. She has just taken her home-baked bread out of the oven. I couldn't help it, I laughed out loud—annoying, I'm sure, those who found the moment moving.

Bright Lights, Big City has a few other women characters. Swoosie Kurtz plays a long-suffering co-worker who covers for Jamie and offers him maternal aid and comfort, getting nothing in return—not even the bagel he promises to bring her from the deli around the corner. Frances Sternhagen plays her standard role, the frigid old-maid librarian type who runs the fact-checking unit where Jamie works. (The men enjoy speculating on whether she urinates standing up and conclude that she doesn't pee at all.) And Tracy Pollan plays a sweet young co-ed, untouched by the evil of the big city, who doesn't mind when a totally wrecked Jamie calls her up in the middle of the night to pour out his sorrows.

I'd like to say that seldom has so talented a cast of actresses been forced to play such a miserable array of moth-eaten female roles, but *Bright Lights, Big City* is no worse than most movies that present a self-indulgent, self-pitying WASP male view of the world. Which is most movies.

Joyce Chopra (*Smooth Talk*) was the director of *Bright Lights* when it started filming a year ago. After three weeks of shooting, she was fired and James Bridges hired. Perhaps a filmmaker with a feminist sensibility just couldn't do justice to the sexist egocentricity of Jay McInerney's novel. If so, she is to be congratulated. Joyce certainly couldn't have done any worse by Jamie than male directors have been doing by women characters all these years.

A defender of *Bright Lights* might argue that women, for the most part, come off as much nicer and better adjusted characters than the men in this movie. That's true. But that's not the point. If these nice, well-adjusted characters aren't created as real, complete human beings with a full range of (even negative) emotions, they are meaningless and insulting. Feminine stock figures just aren't acceptable any more. I'd much rather have a messed-up loser of a woman who looks and acts like a real woman than any number of plaster saints.

And that's why *High Tide*, the new film by Gillian Armstrong, is such a revelation. It does precisely what Hollywood seems incapable of doing. It tells, without glamor or melodrama, of the lives and loves of three totally believable and completely ordinary, working-class women, none of them angels.

The hero of *High Tide* is Lilli (Judy Davis), a burned-out back-up singer for a third-rate Elvis impersonator, Lester (Frankie J. Holden). Lilli does a decent job with her shoo-wops as she prances around stage in a green and purple strapless gown. And she gets along well enough with two co-singers. But Lilli refuses to treat her fake King like a real monarch. She tweaks Lester's male authority once too often and is fired. Her ancient Valiant thereupon conks out, and she finds herself stranded in a poor seaside town called, ironically enough, Eden.

With not enough money to fix her car, and no job prospects, Lilli takes a downspin less flashy than Jamie's, but just as painful. A young surfer girl named Ally (Claudia Karvan) finds Lilli, drunk on Dewars, croaking a Dylan tune from the floor of the trailer park bathhouse and helps Lilli back to her "caravan." The two become friends. And for friendship of another variety, Lilli takes a fisherman, Mick (Davis's husband, Colin Friels), as her lover. Lilli even finds an entertainment job of sorts when the owner of the local pub convinces her to work as a private party and club night stripper. It's a job she recognizes as hitting bottom. But bottom is not a place she is surprised at visiting.

At its lowest point, the tide begins to build again. And so it is with Lilli. Her life comes full circle on the coastline of New South Wales. Her slow descent started more than ten years earlier with the death of her young husband and reverses with a rediscovery of love and commitment, not in her love for a man, but in her reunion with her daughter.

When her husband died, Lilli had taken flight, leaving her young daughter in the care of her mother-in-law, Bet (Jan Adele). A free-wheeling, nomadic life and a lot of booze served to dull the pain, but both losses were always with her, if seldom acknowledged. Now it's all come flooding back, with the discovery that the sturdy young surfer girl who had helped her up from the bathroom floor is her daughter.

It sounds like a soap opera, doesn't it? And it is, in the same way life is a soap opera. *High Tide* never feels like

Lilli (Judy Davis) on the skids in High Tide.

cheap melodrama, however, because Gillian Armstrong is never trifling or lurid in the way she tells her story. And Armstrong's relentless honesty as a director has inspired her lead actors to luminous performances.

Judy Davis, who first worked with Armstrong in *My Brilliant Career*, is an unequivocal Lilli. When life dealt her the proverbial crushing blow by striking down her husband, she wasn't strong and noble. She didn't hang onto her baby and forge a new life for them both. Faced with a fight-or-flight confrontation with sorrow and responsibility, she ran. She's still running. Driven by guilt and pain and scotch, she keeps moving, hurting herself and others. And it's getting harder and harder for her to pretend that what she leads is an "adventurous, brave kind of life."

Davis shows us the instability and bitterness of this woman. But she also shows us her power. In her own way, Lilli is very much a survivor. She's tough and spirited, and honorable enough not to bilk the car mechanic who trusts her to use her car while she earns the rest of the money for her repair bill.

Davis's performance is so mysterious, yet so whole-hearted, that I was mesmerized. Her Lilli isn't lovable. People on the skids usually aren't. But it's hard not to be moved by her. And as haggard and used up as she looks, the beauty of this chalk-white, frizzy-haired woman is enough to take your breath away.

Claudia Karvan, as Ally, also gives a fine performance. She seems so young and innocent as she exchanges flat-faced kisses with her first boyfriend, but she becomes an adult before the viewer's eyes. She is twelve going on fifty— wise now to life's pain and complexity, but still open to its full impact.

But the most impressive performance in *High Tide* has got to be the screen debut of Jan Adele as Bet. Well past her own child-bearing years, Bet is by no means a compulsively maternal woman. She never asked to raise a second family, although she's done a crackerjack job of it with limited resources. She is clearly devoted to her granddaughter but also cares about fulfilling her own needs. Bet is no self-abnegating granny with a starched apron and a stern expression. And I suspect that Bet has never baked a loaf of bread in her life. This is a vital, rugged woman who works hard and plays hard. By day, Bet toils in fish-packing plant and sells soft-serve ice cream from a bright pink truck. By night, she clowns and cuddles with her lover, enjoys partying with friends, and (like the daughter-in-law she despises) hangs onto her dreams of show business, singing in local talent competitions.

At this point, you might be picturing some has-been floozy, of the type too often played by Shelley Winters. Scratch that image. It's just your Hollywood-induced ageism showing. Bet is at no time portrayed as a pathetic or self-deluded woman who never learned to act her age. She knows who she is and how old she is. She's happy with both.

What a liberating and inspiring portrait of a woman this is! Here is a woman who is no longer young, whose pear-shaped body is a good fifty pounds over the fashionable limit. She is nonetheless physically strong and joyously sexual. Besides her regular lover, Col, she takes delight in a one-night stand with a country-western singer passing through town—a delight that is obviously mutual. When, on the morning after, Col rams the empty designer truck of his rival, Country Joe is angry, but freely concedes that his night with Bet was worth a few dents.

Bet brings passion to her parenting as well. She views the reappearance of Lilli as a threat to Ally's happiness, as well as her own. And she doesn't take that threat lightly. She is quite willing to come to blows with her daughter-in-law to keep her from hurting Ally. But she is also a woman who knows, and accepts, the call of blood between mother and child.

But it isn't Lilli who tells Ally she is her mother; it is Mick, the fisherman. Lilli, frightened by his intensity and need, has already dumped him. Mick is back to being an unattached single dad when he wheels his young daughter into the local store, sees Ally, and tells her the identity of her mother. Why does he do it? Is it an accident? Is it a spiteful impulse? Does Mick want to tie Lilli to this place? Or does he, devoted father that he is, merely want to bring mother and child together again? Armstrong doesn't tell us. And Friels, gifted actor that he is, let's us see all of these and more play through Mick's kindly face.

Armstrong doesn't stint on her male characters, but it is her women you'll remember most. To see three such believable women in one movie is truly remarkable, and might have been impossible were it not for the three talented women behind the camera. *High Tide* was a collaborative effort led by Armstrong, screenwriter Laura Jones, and producer, Sandra Levy. The story is the product of all three of their energies and imaginings.

Originally, they wanted to avoid an all-female story. They had, at first, planned Lilli to be a *male* character. But after a re-write, the screenplay still didn't work. So with very few changes, the central figure was changed to a woman. "We thought we'd have to change the script," Armstrong recently admitted. "But that turned out to be a sexist idea. We didn't have to change it at all."

Davis adds that she thinks that Lilli is such "a strong, complex woman" precisely because "she was originally written as a man." Davis was so pleased with her role that she has proposed, half-seriously, that all women's parts be written for men "and then changed."

The idea is less distressing than it sounds. If men and all of us women who have been conditioned by the same limited images of female lives have such a hard time imagining women as strong, imperfect heroes, maybe imagining them first as men or, if you prefer, multi-faceted but genderless human beings, would help us stave off future generations of cinematic plaster saints and mannequins.

I remember reading an essay by Dorothy L. Sayers once in which she relates, with wry amusement, the admiration of a male reader for the way she handled her male characters. He wanted to know how she'd managed to get it right. Sayers writes, "I replied that I had coped with this difficult problem by making my men talk, as far as possible, like ordinary human beings."

If the men of Hollywood could only see the wisdom of that approach in reverse! If they would only give us women who are just "ordinary human beings," it would be a real pleasure to go to the movies. As it is, we have the brilliant career of Gillian Armstrong to hearten us. We can look at *High Tide* and say, "Yes. This is what women look like. This is what women act like. This is who—or part of who—we are."

I've Heard the Mermaids Singing

Sheila McCarthy's Siren Song

I'm always eager to see the latest first feature by a woman director. Well, almost always. If I was less than eager to see Patricia Rozema's movie *I've Heard the Mermaids Singing*, it's only because word of its lofty purpose preceeded it. The title, from T. S. Eliot, was daunting enough. Then I heard that the movie was actually a religious allegory about the nature of creation, and my heart sank. Spread that kind of word about a movie and people like me will stay away in droves.

And that would be a real shame, because *Mermaids* is a warm little film, imaginative and funny, built upon a lead performance that should not be missed.

Polly (Sheila McCarthy) is a very nice, fairly attractive woman who is sound in mind and body. And yet, she is (as Rozema has described her) "someone you wouldn't talk to at a dinner party." There is, after all, something uncomfortably vague about this woman. She is bashful (often to the point of being unable to put together a complete sentence in conversation), and she is clumsy (as if she entered a gawky stage at age thirteen and never managed to find her way out again). A former employer dubbed her "organizationally impaired," which is as good a name for it as any. Although she dresses sedately, almost severely, there is a wildness about Polly. Her carrot-red hair looks like she cuts it at home with school scissors. It sticks out in odd (not fashionably punk) little spikes, adding a lunatic touch to her spaced-out demeanor.

Polly is thirty-one, and has lived alone since the death

of her parents ten years earlier. Perhaps she has lived too long in her own company to retain all of her social skills. She has had "boyfriends," but recognizes herself as "a spinster or something." She leads a frugal existence in her "bachelorette" apartment, eating her dinners (of canned peas and saltine crackers) at the stove while her cat snacks on the countertop nearby.

Sounds like a sad life. That's because many similar films have played similar characters for pathos, inviting us to believe that a life like Polly's isn't worth living. The screenwriters of such stories usually devise a tear-jerking suicide following an aborted affair with a heartless cad. The alternative scenario calls for a slow, downward slide into alcoholism or insanity.

By far and away the most common representation of the single woman in films is as the Shriveled-Up Spinster. She starts out shriveled and continues to shrivel throughout the movie, until she collapses into nothingness. As a symbol of society's contempt for nonconforming (unmarried, child-free) women, she is so widely accepted that she is the stereotype of choice for portraying women who live alone. Polly would have undoubtedly gotten just such a treatment in a Hollywood movie.

Rozema, who wrote her own script, never stoops to such idiocy. In fact, the best thing about *Mermaids* is that Rozema, without romanticizing Polly, shows us how rich Polly's solitary, quirky existence is. There is magic in this woman, in the photographs she takes of things she likes, and even more so in her exhilarating fantasy life. She flies over the city. She walks on water. She communes with mermaids. Only a woman who, deep down, loves herself could bless her dreams this way. And because we see Polly's love of her life and her self, we love and admire, rather than pity, her. By allowing us into Polly's lively imagination, Rozema insures that we won't dismiss her heroine as a geek and a loser. We see her as the beautiful and unique hero of her own story.

Patricia Rozema, director of I've Heard the Mermaids Singing.

It's the story Polly is given to tell, and not the characterization, that is almost the undoing of this heartwarming women's film. It is when *Mermaids* delves into grand themes that it overreaches itself. I could easily have watched two hours of Sheila McCarthy taking photographs and escaping into daydreams. I found it less easy to watch Rozema's lessons, presented through Polly's experiences, on the world of Art.

It all starts when Polly lands a temp job at the Church Gallery, where her boss, Gabrielle St. Pere (Paule Baillargeon), creates a big impression on her. Gabrielle, or the Curator as Polly calls her, is everything our heroine isn't: wealthy, intellectual, fashionably dressed, and very cool and sophisticated. She is, at times, a pretentious and arrogant woman, but at least she has the saving grace of sensing when she's being obnoxious. And she likes Polly. She even gives Polly a permanent part-time job as her "person Friday." Befriending Polly makes her a more likable character, even if her affection for Polly *is* nine-tenths amused condescension.

As chic and cosmopolitan as the Curator usually appears to Polly, there are a few things that can shake even her considerable dignity. The presence of Gabrielle's sometime lover, Mary Joseph (Ann-Marie MacDonald) blows her cool like nothing else. A kiss from Mary is enough to leave Gabrielle almost as organizationally impaired as Polly. But most of the time the Curator efficiently promotes and sells modern artwork. She knows all the buzz words and drops them easily enough. In a conversation with an art critic of her acquaintance, terms like "oblique pragmatism" roll off her tongue with practiced ease.

What doesn't come as easily is her own artistic expression. Gabrielle's deepest melancholy stems from her fear that she will never create a work of lasting beauty. Polly, for whom creativity is a natural, open expression of her life, isn't sure why the Curator experiences such artistic angst, but she would definitely like to do what she can to alleviate it.

At the end of her birthday party, a drunken Gabrielle gives Polly a peek at one of her paintings. (It looked like an x-ray light box to me, but) Polly is thrilled by it. The square expanse of white light is an image Polly doesn't need to "pretend to like." Our hero would like nothing better than to take an active role in promoting the happiness of the woman she has come to love. And since she can think of no good reason for the Curator to be so shy about her fine work, Polly brings the painting to the gallery where it garners critical raves from the Toronto art establishment.

It is this act of devotion that hastens the movie's crisis, along with Gabrielle's inadvertent cruelty to her assistant. Inspired by her role in the Curator's success, Polly gets up the courage to share her photographs with the curator. Too shy to show them to her directly, Polly instead mails several of her favorite photos to Gabrielle under a "pseudo name." Not knowing who they are by, Gabrielle is brutal in her dismissal. "Trite made flesh," she scoffs. And Polly, who had always loved her pictures, is now devastated to find them judged worthless by someone she loves.

The Curator's judgment is cutting, but is it right? Mary Joseph, the dark, attractive lesbian, represents the healthy, less judgmental (that is to say, Rozema's) view of art. When Mary hears Polly parrot Gabrielle's harsh assessment of one of her photos, Mary rebukes her. "Can't you just like it, or not like it, and leave it at that?...What's *good*? What if it's a shot of someone this photographer loves to distraction?— Isn't that a *good* thing?"

Of course it is. And it is something Polly knew all along, until the Curator's superior knowledge brings her own positive instincts into question. Mary validates Polly's own feelings about creation. Earlier, in one of her fantasies, Polly expounds on her philosophy of "relativism" and cautions her lady friend, played in her dream by Gabrielle, against a "right way" to approach creativity—or human relationships.

The Curator's "right way" is the product of too much

exposure to the rigid pomposities of Capital-A Art. It causes her to be false to the two women who love her. When Polly sees that her goddess is a false one, the movie's emotional confrontation occurs. Unfortunately, it is at this point that the movie completely falls apart. I mean badly.

I wish Rozema hadn't tried to do so much in this movie. Lampoons of the art world are plentiful, and often handled better than in *Mermaids*. And they seem so unnecessary. High Art is, after all, its own best parody. What is so much rarer is the portrayal of the woman loner in a positive light. And heaven knows there are precious few positive images of lesbians on film. If Rozema had devoted more of her movie to the relationships of her three female leads, *Mermaids* would have pleased me more.

I prefer not to think of *Mermaids* as a treatise into the nature of Art. And I certainly refuse to spend much time contemplating it as a religious allegory. Although such an interpretation is certainly possible, I found Rozema's extended metaphor—"the Church Gallery" is where The Curator (i.e., The Creator), Ms. St. Pere (i.e., Holy Father) controls creativity, tempered only by the earthly influences of Mary/Joseph—to be a needless distraction.

It is far better to celebrate this movie (and it *does* deserve celebrating) as a joyous portrayal of the spinster and the lesbian. This film is, without doubt, female-identified and ultimately very positive and loving. Forget about the allegory and the high-flown art philosophy, and this film may well enchant you. And Sheila McCarthy, as Polly, is *such* a delight that you'll surely feel like taking her home with you. When the videotape is released, that is undoubtedly what many women will do.

The Allnighter

Blame It on Mom

I've always thought (and I say this as a child-free woman)
that it is grossly unfair the way parents, and especially
mothers, get *all* the blame for the way their children act. You
know the kind of thing I mean: "Ted is an ax-murderer of
young girls—his mother must have been a constant nagger
who dominated him unmercifully." But once in a while it
really *is* fair to blame a mother for the way her child acts.
The Allnighter is proof. In this truly bad film, Tamar Simon
Hoffs directs her daughter Susanna Hoffs in her "motion
picture debut." And the way Susanna acts should fill
Tamar's heart with guilt and remorse for the rest of her days.

Maybe I'm being too hard on Mom, but I don't think so.
I've seen Susanna Hoffs in her better-known role as lead
singer for the all-woman rock-and-roll band The Bangles in
several rock videos. When filmed with co-Bangles Debbi and
Vicki Peterson and Michael Steel, Susanna has shown herself
to possess great energy and charm, as well as a kind of sultry
innocence. In short, star quality. In *The Allnighter*, Hoffs
shows no quality of any kind. She is awkward and dull. And
a lot of the blame must go to her mother as director, co-
screenwriter, and producer.

Part of the problem may be that mothers do not necessarily see their daughters as others see them. Hence,
we have a bad piece of casting waiting to happen. In *The
Allnighter*, Susanna Hoffs plays Molly Morrison, the shy,
innocent valedictorian of the graduating class of Pacifica
College. (Sounds like the perfect role for a rock-and-roll
queen with a sexy image, right?) Molly is having trouble

133

concentrating on her valedictory speech. This presumed virgin is suffering from deep dejection over completing four years of college without one big romance (or small, hot affair). Given the hedonism of her peers, Molly has good reason for her despondency.

Pacifica is the standard teen flick college. The movie's opening makes student priorities quite clear. Gina (Joan Cusack), one of Molly's beach house roommates and a budding filmmaker, wanders from classmate to classmate, sticking her video camera in their faces and demanding to know "what they got out of four years at Pacifica." You can guess the answers: sex, drugs, surfing, sex, football, alcohol, and sex. Even the class nerd (female) indicates that the most important thing she learned was "the true meaning of 69."

I will admit that young adult bacchananlia is not my idea of entertainment and never was. But a teen sexploitation flick can be, at least, visually interesting, have its fun moments, and even sometimes make a point or two about the challenges of growing up. Directors Amy Heckerling (*Fast Times at Ridgemont High*) and Martha Coolidge (*Valley Girl*) have proved this. Tamar Simon Hoffs only proves that teen sexploitation can truly be as dull and pointless as it sounds.

Here is a rundown of the plot of *The Allnighter*. Molly and her roomies and best friends Gina and Val (DeDee Pfeiffer) plan a farewell dinner of lasagna (complete with marijuana substituting for the standard oregano) for their male buddies Killer (James Anthony Shanta) and C.J. (John Terlesky). C.J. and Killer are graduating seniors who have spent their academic careers surfing and calling one another "Dude." C.J. looks like a *Playgirl* centerfold but is supposed to be a brilliant pre-law student on his way to legal training in Boston. (Heaven help us!) Killer is a brain-fried philosopher who picks his toes and says things like "When the Moon is in the Second Wave." The happy group had planned on attending the senior blow-out fiesta together after dinner.

Complications arise. Val's fiancé, a self-centered Valley Boy more interested in career advancement than romance, comes to town and demands the sole attention of his woman. C.J., who refuses to admit his attraction to Molly, is nonetheless jealous when a thirty-five-ish rock-and-roller, Mickey (Michael Ontkean), stops by the girls' beach house for old time's sake—he had once lived there himself—and dances with Molly.

Molly follows the pouting C.J. to the fiesta but is unable to keep his attention from straying to a frisky blonde. In her own snit, she runs home to brood, strip, and grind her hips (in a manner that makes it clear she is *no* novice to the highly suggestive performance of the well-timed pelvic thrust) to the strains of Lady Soul singing "Respect." She then drapes herself in rhinestones, slithers into a short pink dress, and heads for the town's high-class hotel to throw herself at the more mature Mickey. Mickey refuses Molly's advances and, in a predictable bedroom farce scene, pushes Molly out on his balcony when his old fiesta sweetheart, who happens to be Molly's academic advisor (Kaaren Lee), shows up for a sexual reconciliation.

Molly calls Gina (on a phone conveniently located on the balcony) for help. When Gina and Val come to the rescue, they are confused for "working girls" and busted. Molly shows how intelligent and resourceful a class egghead really is by wandering around helplesssly, unable to locate money or assistance in freeing her pals. C.J. eventually comes to the rescue and the two convince mean Sergeant MacLeish (Pam Grier—as beautiful as ever, but totally wasted in this cameo part) to let Gina and Val go. When freed, Val breaks up with her outraged fiancé, and she and Gina claim their jailhouse days as "the best [they've] ever had," and profess their friendship and mutual admiration. Meanwhile, Molly goes to C.J.'s place and finds him in a towel loincloth, fresh from the shower. The two fall into bed (*without* professing their friendship or mutual admiration). After some mute simulated sex, the two show up late for graduation and Molly gives her impromptu valedictory speech on the value of experience. Closing credits.

My parroting of *The Allnighter*'s plot should indicate that, story-wise, this film is no better and no worse than scores of others. It is more a matter of what Tamar Simon Hoff has done, or failed to do, with her material. Where we *should*, at least, feel the warmth and loyalty between the three young women, we feel nothing. They seem uncomfortable and distanced from each other.

When Molly tries to escape Mickey's balcony by climbing off in high heels she is unused to, it is played for neither laughs nor suspense. I kept thinking of how funny that scene could have been (think of Lucy Ricardo in the same situation) or scary (think of Eva Marie Saint hanging off a presidential nose in *North by Northwest*) with some decent acting and direction. But, sadly, Tamar and her daughter never seem to get involved with their material or their audience. They go through the motions as if the film were entitled *The Sleepwalker*.

At my most cynical, I'd say both mother and daughter wanted nothing more than some fast money, making a movie they both knew was trash, just to cash in on Susanna's rock fame. In a more merciful mood, I'd say both are at an early stage of learning their filmcraft and will undoubtably do better next time. They could hardly do worse.

The financial bottom line may explain why these particular women made this particular film, but I wonder if the same explanation holds true for other female schlock directors. Outside of the field of independent filmmaking, especially in the areas of nonfiction film and animation, there are still shockingly few movies directed by women. When a woman does show up as *auteur* of a film, it is usually a piece of teen-audience junk. Amy Hecklerling directed *National Lampoon's European Vacation*, Martha Coolidge directed National Lampoon's *Joy of Sex*. Even worse, Amy Jones (with the collusion of screenwriter Rita Mae Brown) made *The Slumber Party Massacre*.

Why do women do it? Maybe they really like these films. Maybe they feel some kinship with the frustrated adolescent. After all, women know how difficult it is to gain your independence in a world that refuses to respect you like a real adult. That *could* be the reason, but somehow I doubt it. More likely, this is another of those sick jokes the boys in Hollywood like to play. So, girlie, you want to make a movie, here's just the property for you—*Surf-Bunny Chainsaw Murderer in Outer Space*. You don't *want* to make a movie like that? And I thought you *wanted* to be a director!

Once in a while women directors take such dreck and manage to subvert it into something worth watching, but not often enough. More often they are subverted by the material, making something that glorifies violence and/or substance abuse, objectifies women, and trivializes human relations as much as any man-made movie. I find the fact that *The Allnighter* is the first mother-daughter film I've ever seen *very* depressing. Avoid it at all costs.

Back at the start of the 70s, in the joy of my newfound feminism, I remember how wonderful it was to read books by women for the first time. Reading *Tell Me a Riddle*, *Small Changes*, and *Diving into the Wreck* was, as they say, a revelation. I can't describe how hurt and betrayed I felt the first time I read a bad book by a woman, a novel that wasn't just horribly written but lied about women as well. Well, illusions are meant to be shattered. And *The Allnighter* is the perfect shatterer when it comes to movies. It's a sad fact we all need to face: women, too, can create 100 percent Grade-A Hollywood crap.

Women Together and Divided

Outrageous Fortune

Inventing Women as Buddies

Women aren't friends to one another. You'd accept that statement as gospel if you believed half of what you saw on television and in the movies. But, the facts are, as we all know, almost the opposite. Women treasure their close, nurturing friendships with one another—and always have. So why is Hollywood so out of touch with reality?

In my more paranoid moods, I see this as a male conspiracy to divide and conquer women. At other times I see the phenomenon as a more benign problem: a form of they-don't-know-any-better egotism. It follows, after all, that any group that controls the culture is going to see itself as the center of the universe. Therefore, movies and television produced by, written by, and directed by men are bound to show the actions of all of society's "others" revolving around WASP males.

There have been Hollywood movies (*Stage Door*, 1937, has always been a personal favorite) that allowed women their friendships, but almost all of them were made before the baby boom. Television shows (*I Love Lucy*, 1951-59, and *Laverne and Shirley*, 1976-83) sporadically showed love and loyalty between women friends. But such media relationships are indeed few and far between, and were hardest to come by during the time I was growing up in the 50s and 60s. (Luckily I had the movies of the 30s on TV as role models of women's camaraderie.) Most contemporary popular culture during the post-war family years, and even now, shows women turning to, and revolving around, men as their sole source of comfort, companionship, and sexual heat, not to mention financial support. When seen together on the screen, most women spend their time either talking about men or competing over men. We're never really there with—or for—one another.

Since the mid-70s, the culture has paid lip service to feminism by allowing women more active roles, sometimes in support of one another. A few movies, like *Julia* (1977), try hard to do justice to our friendships. The story of Lillian Hellman's friendship with another woman may move us to tears, but brilliant performances by Jane Fonda and Vanessa Redgrave cannot completely fill in the blank spots in Alvin Sargent's screenplay. We learn much more about Hellman's relationship with Dashiell Hammett than we do about her relationship with the title character. Even in films *about* our friendships, men always seem to end up right smack in the middle of things.

Look at the 1985 sudser, *Just Between Friends*. The title certainly sounds promising. The friends of the title are played by Mary Tyler Moore and Christine Lahti. The story goes that two women, one a homemaker, the other a career woman, meet at an aerobics class and quickly recognize in each other a soul sister. The two become best friends, but (what a coincidence!) they both happen to be in love with the same man, Mary's hubby, played by Ted Danson.

Ted conveniently dies a third of the way into the movie, leaving the two gals to duke it out over his memory. Allan Burns (director, co-producer, and writer) allows the women to salvage their friendship, but only after the standard re-criminations and guilt-ridden pleas. Dear, dead Ted is still the compelling presence. The final scene shows Mary and

Christine sitting on a sofa, holding Ted's newborn son while they watch home movies of Ted's smiling face in what is meant to be a touching valediction. Yeech!

It's hard to count the number of ways in which *Just Between Friends* is phony and ridiculous. The number of contrivances and coincidences alone make it a classic of the unbelievable. The most insidious thing about the film's phallocentricity is the way it invites us to believe that these two women are destined to be friends precisely because they belong to the same man—as if they were sister-wives in an old-fashioned Mormon household. As the advertising slogan points out, these are "Two Friends with Nothing in Common...Except the Man They Love."

Mary and Christine not only have nothing in common, they seem to have few resources for friendship outside of their "other woman" counterpart. Burns implies that these two women have no other close female friendships. Yet their ties to one another are almost mystical. The boy-child even provides a blood-tie between the two. There is *one* other significant friendship for the two women. *Another man*, played by Sam Waterston. And they seem to be on the road to sharing *him* at the end of the movie!

That's Hollywood's view of female friendship. And now they've given us another view, in what the producers have touted as the "first genuine female buddy action comedy." It's supposed to be a new kind of movie, but it looks like the same old mythology to me. In fact, it could have used the same slogan as *Just Between Friends*, because this, too, is a movie about "two friends who have nothing in common... but the man they love." *Outrageous Fortune* is the name of it. It stars Bette Midler and Shelley Long, and it's packing them in all across the country.

Shelley Long plays Lauren, a consistently unemployed actress who works in a costume and souvenir shop when she's not taking her ballet, fencing, or acting lessons. Lauren makes up for in training what she lacks in talent and professional experience. She's studied every possible theatrical

142

skill, but still can't get a job in the theater. Her parents, sick of footing the bill for it all, have banished her from their uptown apartment building. But that doesn't keep Lauren from begging for money via the security intercom/ video monitor at the front door.

Lauren wants more tuition money. This time it is to study with famed Russian coach, Stanislov Korzenowski (Robert Prosky). With money from Dad (thrown from a window, since Lauren's Mom won't let her in the door) she rushes to the auditions. Once there, she babbles vocal exercises until her concentration is shattered by a loud, foulmouthed redhead who wanders into Korzenowski's outer office to use the phone. The redhead, Sandy (Midler), also claims to be an actress (her last screen credit was *Ninja Vixens*). So when Lauren insults her in the most condescending manner, Sandy decides to audition for Korzenowski, too, just to get Ms. La-de-dah's goat.

Sandy, who tickles the teacher's fancy, not only gets in, she even gets a scholarship. Lauren is outraged and resentful, but must content herself with a little low-grade verbal sniping, which Sandy returns as good as she gets. Then something happens that throws the two women together: A man.

Both women have the same lover. He is a single girl's prayer (later nightmare) named Michael, played by Peter Coyote. Michael tells them both that he is a single elementary school teacher who'd like to get married. Both of them buy his blarney, and live in blissful hope that they've finally found their one and only. Neither knows of the other's existence. That is, until Mr. Love's Dream is blown up, and both women show up at the morgue to mourn and identify the remains. Lauren is aghast at the idea that Michael could sleep with Sandy. And Sandy fails to see what any man could see in Lauren. Both refuse to believe Michael was "boffing" (as Sandy likes to call it) someone they despise.

Both claim the dear departed as their exclusive property until they get a closer look at the body. Then neither one wants it. The face is gone, but the lower torso is still intact. And from the size of the equipment (I told you this was phallocentric mythology), the two conclude that Michael is still alive. If he's alive, he has a lot of explaining to do. The two take off after Mr. Two-timer, resolved to find him, if for no other reason than to make him choose between them.

At this point, the plot takes off in all kinds of silly directions involving the CIA, and the FBI, and ye olde Threat to Life on This Planet. I have no real objections to rookie screenwriter Leslie Dixon's story line. It's ridiculous, but acceptably so for a comedy-adventure. My complaints are with the way Sandy and Lauren are portrayed.

These are types, not characters. Lauren, with her stiff carriage and Laura Ashley look, is the blonde upper-class priss. Sandy, with her mincing toddle and trashy flash, is your average henna-haired, working-class slut figure. These are both women who are more concerned about breaking a nail than falling off a cliff. And when they're running for their life, they can't help but stop to try on a "darling" new outfit.

Perhaps this kind of characterization is to be expected in a comedy-adventure, but I don't think so. Male comedy-adventure buddy films like *48 Hours* may show two men with very little in common, but they do it without trivializing maleness or reducing their characters to stock figures. And they don't feel the need to suggest that men become friends because of a woman or not at all. Lauren and Sandy, like Mary and Christine, appear to live isolated lives until their jealousy over Michael brings them together. Leslie Dixon, granddaughter of Dorothea Lange, obviously can't manage the same respect for her sex as male screenwriters consistently show. Perhaps that is why she (who has been quoted as denying that there is a "general prejudice against women" as screenwriters) is one of the hottest authors in Tinseltown today.

I don't want to come down too hard on *Outrageous Fortune*. It does, at least, let these women (once they find out that their man doesn't want either one of them) become supportive friends. And if you're going for priss versus slut stereotypes, you couldn't cast better than with the over-educated Diane Chambers and the raunchy but Divine Ms. M. The contrast and interplay between Shelley Long and Bette Midler is often uncomfortable but hilarious. These two women are fabulous together. And Coyote, who has always been my idea of Love's Dream, too, is wonderfully oily as the bad guy who's a great lay.

I can be as much a sucker as any other movie-goer. I had fun watching two women save the world and find a friend in one another. When Lauren foils her evil lover and then taunts "Nine years of ballet, Asshole!" I laughed and cheered along with everyone else. The final shot of Lauren and Sandy, hands raised together (fading to strains of Annie Lennox singing "The Last Time") is enough to make me leave a theater feeling mighty chipper. But it's not enough to erase my misgivings about Hollywood's new-fangled women's friendship after I got home.

Deep, abiding, mutually supportive friendship between women is something the male culture doesn't like to think about. It makes them uncomfortable to see it in a film or hear about it in studies like Shere Hite's, which show that the majority of women surveyed got most of their emotional sustenance from other women. Insecure creatures that they are, men can't bear to think that they aren't the be-all and end-all of a woman's emotional life. They might reason that if women don't need men for *everything*, it's only a short leap to the blasphemous idea that women might not need men at all.

It's good to see, with the release of movies like *Just Between Friends* and *Outrageous Fortune*, that Hollywood is finally recognizing with some regularity that women can be friends. Now, if they'd only admit the frequency and depth of those friendships! Our relationships with one another are important to us. But, regardless of what the movies like to show, nine times out of ten, women's friendships have nothing to do with our relationships with men.

So far, movies have only given us partial permission to be buddies. They seem to be saying, "You can be friends, but only when men aren't around." Or, to put it more bluntly, it's almost as if the men who make the movies are telling us, "Sure, you gals can be friends—over our dead bodies." I can almost hear Bette Midler, a tough-girl sneer on her face, reply to that one: "Hey! Don't give us any ideas, buddy boys!"

Crimes of the Heart

Sisterhood Is Pixilated

Not many playwrights, especially women playwrights, experience an initial and immediate triumph like Beth Henley's. While Henley did spend a few dues-paying days in student and regional theater, her first professionally produced play was a black/absurdist/sentimental comedy called *Crimes of the Heart*, which started out regionally, moved to off-off-Broadway, and eventually found its way to the Great White Way. The play won several awards in 1981, including the Pulitzer Prize and the New York Drama Critics Circle Award. Since her smash debut, Beth Henley has moved on to Hollywood with mixed results. Her *Nobody's Fool*, directed by Evelyn Purcell, opened last month nationwide and closed so quickly in Boston that slow-moving moviegoers like myself didn't even get a chance to see it. But if *Nobody's Fool* failed to find its audience, there seems little doubt that Henley's own adaption of *Crimes of the Heart* will fare considerably better at the box office, if for no other reason than that it features three of the hottest female stars currently working in Hollywood.

Crimes is the story of the three Magrath sisters, reunited by family misfortune at the family homestead, a crumbling gingerbread Victorian in Hazelhurst, Mississippi. Lenny (Diane Keaton), the eldest sister, is a shy and self-conscious spinster who stayed home to care for the grandfather who raised them. "Old Granddaddy" (Hurd Hatfield) is now dying in the local hospital, the victim of a series of strokes, but Lenny has even more pressing worries: the whereabouts and well-being of her sisters.

The three stars of Crimes of the Heart: *Diane Keaton (top), Jessica Lange (bottom), and Cissy Spacek (left).*

Youngest sister Babe (Sissy Spacek) has just been incarcerated for attempted murder in the shooting of her husband of several years, a prosperous lawyer and local politico named Zackery Botrelle (Beeson Carroll). And middle sister Meg (Jessica Lange) is seemingly out of reach, living in L.A. with a disconnected phone and a failed singing career.

It looks like another lousy (and lonely) birthday for poor Lenny. But then Meg comes home, Babe is released on bail, and the three sisters are free to comfort and torment one another again as they have since they were children.

Their childhood was not easy. When they were tiny tykes, their handsome father abandoned the family. Later, in the cellar of the house where they now gather, their mother (who had "had a bad day") abandoned them as well, hanging herself and her pet cat. It wasn't the kind of childhood most likely to promote mental health and sound emotional development. And it didn't. Fact is, the Magrath sisters are, to a woman, utterly charming walking basket cases.

Despite the tragedy of their early lives, Henley doesn't see the Magrath sisters as tragic heroines. Neither does she pity them (or invite us to pity them) for their mental quirks or emotional instability. Henley seems to be saying that there's nothing wrong with a little honestly acquired nuttiness. It is *normalcy*, represented by both the Magrath's shrewish first cousin Chick (Tess Harper—who is fabulous in the role), who has a modern home, husband, two children, and social climbing ways, and by the ambitious and successful Zackery Botrelle, that is seen as incomplete, almost evil.

We could expect many film fans to be uncomfortable with such a view. I think Beth Henley wants us to be uneasy and to experience a variety of emotions at the same moment. She wants us to see life as both sad and hilarious. She encourages us to giggle at death and human misery—and yet recognize their tragic implications.

It's hard to pull off all that in a movie. If the film works, and for the most part it does, it is no thanks to director

Bruce Beresford, who takes a rather ponderous approach to the proceedings, consistently taking wide angle shots when he should take close-ups and close-ups shots when he should share the interaction between his three leads freely.

The relative success of *Crimes of the Heart* belongs instead to Beth Henley's faithfulness to her original play, and even more to the amazing fact that even Hollywood stars can do a good turn of ensemble acting if they put their minds *to* it (and their egos *away* from it). When I first heard that Keaton, Lange, and Spacek were playing the Magrath sisters, I was dismayed (and not just because, as a Mary Beth Hurt fan, I was offended that she was not allowed to reprieve her New York role of Meg).

Rather, I was dismayed because *Crimes of the Heart* is no star vehicle. It is a play, in the great tradition of the theater, that requires a cooperative performance among a trio of actors who each have equal value to the production. This is *not* the approach most often used in Hollywood or very commonly indulged in by stars of the magnitude of Keaton, Lange, and Spacek. But I was very pleasantly surprised. There was no upstaging or scene grabbing that I could notice in this film. These three stars were apparently respectful to and generous with each other. Such a sisterly attitude toward their performance deserves applause and results in some enchanting interplay.

As to individual performances, it is easy to point to Sissy Spacek as outstanding. Her Babe is a balmy innocent, a gracious southern belle who would plug her husband in the belly (she was aiming for his heart) and then offer him a glass of fresh lemonade. She paints polka dots on her toenails and toots a saxophone while wearing a drum majorette's boots and crown. And because of Spacek's absolute sincerity, we don't doubt any of it. With her lawyer, young Barnette Lloyd (David Carpenter), we watch her empty her salted peanuts into her Coke bottle and then munch and sip away as she tells her tale of marital woe and vengeance. Like Barnette, we never question either her eating habits or her actions toward her husband, but we fall in love with this lunatic waif.

Jessica Lange's performance is more enigmatic. Meg suffers from all the self-doubt of the middle sibling and, on top of that, was the first to find her mother's body. She was a wild teenager, breaking the heart—and leg—of Doc Porter (Lange's real-life sweetie, Sam Shepard), the only man she ever loved, during a drunken spree when she refused to evacuate during hurricane Camille. Her singing career has failed, as has her life-long attempts to toughen herself in the face of death and suffering. As a small child she had forced herself to study the gruesome pictures in a medical text called *Diseases of the Skin* and to spend her March of Dimes coins on ice cream, but her toughening program didn't take. As an adult, she was recently institutionalized for attempting to stuff all her money and jewelry into a charity tin in a California store.

Meg's journey home allows her to release herself from the guilt that has haunted her since the desertion of her father. Lange explores this process with beautiful subtlety. The layers of emotion she is able to put into taking a bite of candy or a swig of Old Crow are breathtaking. All the hurt and fear are clearly visible beneath the armor of Lange's long-legged sophistication. If we watch closely we can see her tough punkish energy relax into a growing tenderness toward her sisters and herself. It's an impressive performance.

More problematic is Diane Keaton as Lenny. As the sister who stayed completely tied to home, Lenny needs a more convincing southern accent than Keaton is able to muster. Ms. Keaton does produce an accent of sorts (you haven't lived until you've heard her say "Yay-us"), but it keeps fading in and out. And—I couldn't help myself—in her jumpers and hats Keaton still looked like Annie Hall to me, an Annie gone to seed, living proof of what happens to any woman who dares to dump Woody Allen.

I don't mean to be ungenerous. With her vulnerability

and her wide-legged waddle and flapping hands, Keaton is endearing as Lenny, even when she's not totally convincing. And her performance is not so bad that it detracts from the group performance. She definitely provides something for Spacek and Lange to play off.

Crimes of the Heart is a loving salute to the walking wounded of life. It is about acceptance and family feeling. It is also, on some level, about women releasing themselves, forcibly if need be, from the thralldom of men. Babe frees herself from her husband in a moment of revelation. When Zackery attacks the fifteen-year-old black boy she frolics with in the garage, Babe grabs a gun and at first points it to her own head. Then, in a moment of communion with her lost mother, she realizes that it is her husband and not herself she really wants to destroy. Even the prospect of prison does not faze her after her liberating rejection of Zackery and marriage.

Meg, too, needs to free herself from a man or, more specifically, from her fear of being "choked" by her love for Doc. That fear had caused her to run west. And so, on this return trip, after a one-night stand with an older Doc, Meg is jubilant and not at all "humiliated" when Doc doesn't ask her to run away with him. She realizes that she can care for a man and not be tied to him, a realization that allows her literally to find her voice again.

And Lenny, poor Lenny, had been tied by duty to Old Granddaddy. Her grandfather had convinced her that her "shrunken ovary" was the kind of affliction that made her worthless to all men except him. At one point, Lenny rebukes Meg for calling Old Granddaddy a "miserable, old, bossy man." When Lenny reminds Meg that their grandfather wanted only "the best for us," Meg admits as much, then adds, "But I sometimes wonder what *we* wanted." Henley acknowledges that the soon-expected death of Old Granddaddy will be a liberation for Lenny, allowing her to start her own life, possibly with a once-rejected beau from Memphis.

Wanting an old man dead is not exactly a socially acceptable path to liberation (and neither, for that matter, is sleeping with a married man or shooting your husband), but Beth Henley isn't asking the audience to forgive the Magrath sisters. Their easy, almost joyous, violation of so many taboos is the one aspect of Henley's play that will cause many viewers to loathe this picture. Your level of enjoyment of *Crimes of the Heart* will depend largely on your willingness to accept the Magrath sisters on their own terms.

I was able, nasty feminist that I am, to accept their rebellion when it consisted of acts against patriarchal family and love. The episode of Willie Jay was less easy for me to stomach. Willie Jay is the young black boy who becomes Babe's lover, precipitating the violent confrontation between wife and husband. When Babe tells Meg about Willie Jay, Meg says that she never realized Babe was a "liberal." Babe replies, "I'm not a liberal....I was just lonely!"

Babe is telling the truth. She is not a liberal. And she doesn't appear to have any recognition of how racist and exploitive it was to seduce a black schoolboy. And, although she appears sad at the parting, she also appears to suffer no guilt over the fact that, to avoid scandal, Willie Jay is ripped from his family and shipped off to New York. To face what kind of horrible, lonely life, you might wonder. Well, *we* might wonder, but Babe and her sisters don't seem to give it a second thought.

Apparently, Henley wants to accept this "crime" as easily as all the others. I could not. Perhaps I could *forgive* it, but Henley isn't asking for pardon for her trio of slightly deranged heroines.

In Beth Henley's world there are reasons for everything and method to all our madnesses. Forgiveness doesn't come into it; love and acceptance do. When the Magrath sisters share fistfuls of birthday cake in the film's final scene, they are coming together in a moment of pure celebration of life and sisterly love. It is a magical moment for them. If we, the audience, can accept Lenny and Meg and Babe for exactly who they are, then *Crimes of the Heart* can be magical for us, too.

Working Girls

Just Another Job?

As with so much of the adult world, my first exposure to the concept of prostitution was through the movies. The movie was *Waterloo Bridge*, and I was all of ten years old, watching it on television. Vivian Leigh played Myra, a ballet dancer (so beautiful!) who fell in love with Robert Taylor during World War I. Taylor is shipped off to the front before they can marry, and Myra loses her job with the ballet. Poor and hungry, when she reads that her true love died in the war, she becomes a prostitute to get enough money for food. Everything's pretty hopeless for poor Myra until Taylor (whose death report was a bureaucratic slip-up) returns and claims her hand. But she can't bear the thought of disgracing his noble family name, and rather than confess her horrible sin, she kills herself on the same bridge where they met.

What a story! I cried my little eyes out, and had no idea why. I didn't understand what poor Myra was so upset about. And the circumspect manner in which Hays Code censorship forced Hollywood to deal with a hot topic like prostitution was no help. From what I could tell, her disgrace consisted of some bad fashion decisions (the satiny dress she wore while working wasn't particularly flattering—although it did show her figure off) and her willingness to walk around London arm-in arm with several boisterous British soldiers. Was that something to kill yourself over? Not to me.

Later, after talking it over with friends, I came to understand that "the world's oldest profession" was about more than walking arm-in-arm. But the movies still helped to keep me confused about the terrible sin of it, and its dire consequences. In later hooker movies, the women usually didn't kill themselves, but frequently someone else tried to do the job for them. There was the occasional whore with the heart of gold who managed to go respectable and live happily ever after (see any number of Shirley MacLaine movies), but most of the time prostitutes were portrayed as a self-hating and desperate lot with a short life-expectancy. Streetwalkers had it especially rough. Jack the Ripper johns sliced them up. Their pimps beat them to death. Or, at the very least, they died from an overdose of heroin.

The high-priced call girl didn't frequent back alleys, and her wardrobe was more tasteful and elegant; but according to the movies, her life was almost as depressing and violent. Bree Daniels in *Klute* got out okay. But she had an equally high-priced shrink and the love of an uptight guy to see her through. Simone (Cathy Tyson) in the recent British film *Mona Lisa* had worse luck, but that's because she never really aligned herself with her soft-hearted thug of a champion. Throughout it all, the message seemed to be that fallen women deserved to suffer and die.

The prostitute, strange as it may seem, is one of the great romantic and tragic character types of film. The film mythology about prostitution is an elaborate one, and it has influenced everyone—including feminists. I think this film mythology is one of the reasons so many feminists made the leap between thinking of prostitutes as worthless sinners to thinking of them as the ultimate victims of sexism, without sufficiently recognizing them simply as working women of the sex industry.

Feminist filmmaker Lizzie Borden is trying to do something about that. In her new feature film, *Working Girls*, she explodes much of the existing film tradition about prostitution by showing a day in the life of one prostitute who works in a "middle-class" brothel in Manhattan.

Molly (Louise Smith) starts her day off with a family breakfast shared with her female lover and her lover's daughter. Afterwards she spends some time in her dark-room, developing and evaluating her photographs. Soon it's time to go to work. She bikes to a duplex in the city, has a chat with her co-workers, then starts answering phones and serving clients. Sounds like many a job, and it is. That's precisely Borden's point.

There is nothing thrilling about what Molly does. Neither is there a sense of pervasive danger or excitement. This is sexual work, but (except in the mind of the trick) not erotic. Molly never "comes" at work. And the gaze of Borden's camera reflects the emotional distance of her protagonist from her job. The sensibilities and actions of Borden's players are never heightened for effect. By retaining an almost documentary-like approach to her sensational subject, her directorial viewpoint never panders to the sexual fantasies of her audience. She's trying to cut through the mythology, so her women spend more time checking their watches (a client's time is strictly measured by the half-hour or hour) and changing sheets and towels than talking dirty to their tricks. There *is* a little panting and moaning done, but none of it by our heroines. And under Borden's relentless gaze, the cries of passion uttered by the various johns are pathetic, not provocative.

After seeing *Working Girls*, you realize how very male the viewpoint is in all the films on prostitution you've ever seen. The focus is on the male client or pimp, and his fantasies of sex and power, violence and control, or, in the minority of cases, redemption of the fallen female. The pro-stitute, as the object of those fantasies, is either in sexual heat (or a close approximation thereof) with her wanton sex-uality tantalizingly mixed with fear of being hurt by the more powerful man, or she is a masochistic sex slave too spineless to escape the degradation forced on her by the dominant maleness of her pimp and tricks. Borden turns this male turn-on off by focusing on the women's professional (un-emotional, nonsexual) approach to their work, and on their sense of control and ease with what they're doing.

156

Molly claims to have actually *lost* her fear of men by becoming a prostitute. Her co-worker, Gina (Marusia Zach), agrees. "It's amazing, isn't it? You can handle any man as long as you know what his sexual trip is." And these women definitely know the sexual trips of their clients. Head games and social/hygienic rituals are the biggest part of the job. Sex is a relatively small part. Their work day is filled with the practiced smiles of any service job. They provide their clients with drinks, offer small talk, and ask them about how things are at their jobs. And just like a burned-out flight attendant or a harassed secretary, their attitude toward their job is nine-tenths bored acceptance and one part discontent.

The pay, which is decent and completely unreported to Uncle Sam, is what keeps them at it. It's all a matter of commerce, and anything out of the ordinary costs the trick extra. The poor bozos don't even get what they pay for half the time. (They don't call them tricks for nothing.) One braggart, referred to as "Fagbag Jerry," decides to cap off his visit with a touch of "around the world," but while he compliments Gina on her talented tongue, she has a laugh with Molly over his pale rump. Gina demonstrates to Molly that a moistened finger is a much easier way of making the extra fee. The scene isn't as graphic as it sounds and it is there more to show the women's contempt for the client than to illustrate a kinky sex practice.

Contempt for the boss is also in large supply. Like most workers, Molly and the other women working her shift, Gina and Dawn (Amanda Goodwin), think their boss is a real jerk. They think right. Lucy (Ellen McElduff) is the manager (a.k.a. madam) of the operation. She's up from the ranks, so to speak, but you'd never know it from her dress-for-success summer suit and superior airs. She's not at the house very much—she spends most of her time shopping—but when she's there she enjoys throwing her weight around. She criticizes the women's wardrobes, their housekeeping habits, and the way they staff the phones. With the clientele she is all effusive charm ("What's new and different?" she gushes at them all), but with her employees she is officious and just plain bitchy.

The women ignore her kvetching as much as they can and look for ways to undermine Lucy's authority and profit margin. They cheat the books when she's not there, and side with one another in work conflicts (like when Dawn refuses to serve a trick who won't wear a condom). Lucy sometimes fools herself into thinking that she and her girls are all one big happy family, but Molly and Gina and Dawn aren't fooled. They know who's got the power, and who gets to keep the big bucks at the end of the shift.

As avaricious and overbearing as Lucy is, she is still a far cry from the abusive pimp we usually see on the silver screen. And as confined as that apartment bordello sometimes seems, it *is* a clean and cheerful place, nothing like the inner-city alleyways we are used to seeing as the workplace of the cinematic hooker. In fact, some viewers, feminists included, may find Borden's version of the Life too wholesome and ordinary.

In her attempt to neutralize some of the emotional hype surrounding prostitution, Borden runs the risk of being perceived as promoting prostitution as a viable career path for today's woman. But there's a difference between being nonjudgmental in the way you present your material and actually advocating its content, and Lizzie Borden never crosses the line between the two. Nor does Borden's picture of prostitution negate the fact that women have indeed suffered as prostitutes. That's reality. It's just not the reality that this particular film is trying to present. And even middle-class prostitution is no bed of roses, as Borden shows as the day at the duplex progresses.

Working Girls recognizes, even partially validates, the squeamishness most of us feel about prostitution. It does this in several ways. First, it shows Molly's dealing with tricks who are unclean and unkind (mentally sadistic if not physically brutal). Secondly it introduces a new viewpoint. We get to meet Mary (Helen Nicholas), on her first—and last—day as a working girl. We feel her disgust and fear at what economic need is forcing her to do. Molly has to give her survival tips (e.g., "Don't do *anything* they don't ask you for.") and sisterly support. But Molly's views as a seasoned pro are a far cry from Mary's. To Molly, a "show" (a lesbian performance for the sexual entertainment of the john) is "great" because it means an extra $100 fee. Mary's reaction is closer to sheer terror and isn't wholly a matter of homophobic revulsion.

To Mary, as to most of us, sexual expression has deep and very personal significance. It is impossible for her to think of sex work in the same way as being a hostess at a restaurant (which is what Lucy advertised for in the *Village Voice*). "Do you think he knew I didn't like it?" Mary worries. "Mary, he doesn't *want* to know," Molly assures her.

But the empty embraces and lackluster fantasies of it are not something everyone can stomach. Mary can't. And if we can't, that's okay. But, for now, it *is* acceptable work for Gina and Dawn and many other women. They hope to be doing something else eventually, and Borden's research showed her that prostitution is, for most women, a short-term career path. Tough-talking Dawn is in college and hopes to be a lawyer someday. Gina is saving money to open her own small business. And Molly, our Yale graduate and photographer? She's getting out now.

After working her full shift, Molly is cajoled and browbeaten by Lucy into working a double-shift to cover for another woman. But even for someone inured to the physical grind and the power skirmishes with some of the more unpleasant clients, a double-shift is too much. It leaves Molly feeling exhausted and emotionally exposed. So she checks her money stash, decides it's enough, and bids a less than fond farewell to the boss lady.

It makes for an upbeat ending to see Molly bike through the nighttime streets, stopping at the market for flowers and at the ATM to deposit her ill-gotten gains. The viewer hopes that she means it about getting out. But even if she doesn't, we know she'll be all right. At least as all right as the rest of us.

Assisted by a good central performance by Smith as her Everywoman prostitute, and equally fine photography and writing, Lizzie Borden has done important work here. She is helping to break down the barriers between women working in the sex industry and those of us toiling in other vineyards. And, just as important, she has broken through the mythology of prostitution passed on by decades of American movies.

If only poor Myra could have met Molly or seen this fascinating movie, she might not have jumped in front of that lorry on Waterloo Bridge. And the rest of us, who have watched the "fallen" Myras of the movies, and who so readily sanctioned the self-hatred of their suicides, or the inevitability and poetic justice of their batterings and murders, might not have accepted those deaths as entertainment.

The Witches of Eastwick

Biology is a Devilish Destiny

The translation of a novel into film is usually a frustrating experience for anyone who has read the book. There is a lushness, a depth to prose—the way a writer takes words and our own imaginations and fashions from them detailed characters, story lines, and locales—that just cannot be equaled by the literal simplicity of a Hollywood movie. *The Color Purple* is probably the most heartbreaking example of this. But *The Witches of Eastwick*, the 1984 best-seller by John Updike, is *not* another example. At least not by my standards. Here, Updike's long, deadly dull misogynist tract is transformed into an entertaining, generally misandrist film.

In the book (a nasty piece of work to be avoided like the Evil Eye), three witches, confident in their destructive power after reducing their respective husbands to dust, herbs, and a plasticized placemat, neglect their kids and cavort (with surprisingly little joy) with every stray husband in sight. A new man in town, Darryl Van Horne, provides fresh sexual intrigue and foul-mouthed creative muse for all three.

The coven enjoys hot times in a hot tub with Darryl. But even this relaxing pastime doesn't mellow out these women. They strike squirrels and puppies dead almost accidentally, while human beings, and especially women, suffer their most deliberate and vicious malice.

The coven's climactic act of evil is performed when Darryl enrages them by marrying his young lab assistant (who is the daughter of two of the witches' earlier victims). For this outrage the coven destroys *not* their wayward svengali, but his young, pregnant bride instead. Their curses over a waxen effigy successfully riddle her healthy body with cancer, and she wastes away and dies. At book's end, the three leave Eastwick with new husbands they have conjured up for themselves.

The movie, as written by Michael Cristofer and directed by George Miller (of *Mad Max* fame), uses the same basic elements but changes the focus and the intent completely, successfully turning Updike's repulsive novel on its ear. In the film, three women, all either divorced, widowed, or abandoned by husbands, band together to survive the sexual harassment and social isolation of being female and single in a small town. At an outdoor civic ceremony each woman fervently wishes that the long-winded tirade of a hypocritical right-wing principal be cut short by rain. Yet even when their prayers are answered in a swift and mighty downpour, the women continue to be unaware of their power. Sculptor Alexandra (Cher), cellist and music teacher Jane (Susan Sarandon), and local reporter Sukie (Michelle Pfeiffer) consider themselves unremarkable women, best buddies who get together every Thursday night to eat junk food, drink martinis, and gossip. During one of these nibble-and-bitch sessions the three fantasize about the perfect lover: a dark stranger who would be respectful and understanding, good to talk to, and fun in bed.

The next day, Darryl Van Horne (Jack Nicholson) appears, filling the old Lenox mansion with his pianos and the town of Eastwick with his eccentric presence. The women are charmed and, one by one, they fall under the spell of Darryl's courtly lunacy.

Darryl is one of those dangerous post-feminist fellows who "likes women." "Women are the source—the only power," he claims. (They can, after all, make both babies and the milk to feed them.) Marriage, he admits, is great for men, but death for women. And while that's just the kind of line an 80s guy puts out when he doesn't want to make a commitment, Darryl still talks a good game as a benevolent if slightly wacky lover.

As portrayed by Nicholson in a brazen performance, Van Horne is a strange combination of the Modern Man and the Retrograde Woman. His exercises in role reversal are hilarious, as in his first conquest of Alexandra. He writhes on his bed in a parody of Playmate of the Month porn, smiling seductively. And the dialogue! Although he is speaking of emotional needs, his lines sound exactly like triple-X feminine movie-speak. "Use me," he pleads with Alexandra. "Fill me up. Make it happen. Do it, Alex."

Likewise, when seducing the shy and repressed Jane, the dialogue, while superficially about bringing passion to music, is really about another kind of passion. Jane's increasingly frenzied cello playing to Darryl's torrid piano-thumping culminates in a musical inferno with Jane roughly embracing Darryl in an inverted take-off of that infamous old Tabu ad.

Sound ridiculous? You bet. The movie's early scenes are a brilliant spoof on both traditional female and post-macho male courtship rituals, with Nicholson playing both extremes against the middle of the witches' gentle feminism. The skill of Nicholson's performance is that his "horny little devil" manages to be ludicrous and absolutely convincing, a balancing act that is essential if we are to accept the possibility that three likable women would agree to enter a *menage à quatre* with this maniac.

The fact that the witches *are* so likable and well intentioned is the key to the movie's subversion of Updike. It is also, ironically, the reason Nicholson's Darryl is so much more important to the movie than Updike's Darryl is to the book. Nicholson is absolutely central to *Witches*. Evil is, after all, more compelling than virtue. And Darryl is evil. No doubt about it, he is the devil incarnate.

If the three women's increasing awareness of their power as witches is a source of innocent (silly, madcap) joy to them, their reluctant realization of who and what Darryl is brings them fear and pain. When a conservative local politician, Felicia Gabriel (Veronica Cartwright), starts a witch hunt in the Eastwick paper that she publishes and her tame husband Clyde (Richard Jenkins) edits, Darryl—with a little help from Clyde—destroys her.

It is at this point that the movie starts to fall apart. With no transition to prepare the audience, the film shifts from a light-hearted sex farce to a horror film full of disgusting special effects. This shift intersects with the witches' awareness of the danger Darryl represents. At first they withdraw from him. But when his evil powers are unleashed against their own, they plot to bring him down.

It is wonderful to see three women, newly empowered (even if it is through the sexual awakening of the devil), rejecting evil magic. "You can't use your power to hurt people!" Alex tells Darryl. Van Horne scoffs. Yet despite his threats and attacks, the witch triumvirate continues to align itself with positive energy against male wickedness. Best of all, working together, they beat the devil.

The down side of this quasi-feminist fable is the tacked-on ending that tells us that all three witches had children (*sons*, of course) by the banished satan. Why the filmmakers felt the need to add this absurd element to their story is beyond me. It certainly harks back to the mystical glory-of-motherhood mumbo-jumbo that Darryl spouts early in the movie. But wise up, Cristofer! Do you really think that three intelligent women, two of whom already have nice kids, would carry the Evil Seed to term, knowing the full malevolence of the father's power? In a pig's eye.

Guess biology is still destiny. Even for witches. This unfortunate conclusion to an entertaining film will undoubtedly ruin it for many feminist viewers. Not me, though. I must admit that I still thoroughly enjoyed *The Witches of Eastwick*.

The performances are wonderful. Jack Nicholson is the perfect devil, grotesque and adorable, and I say this as someone who normally loathes his screen presence: Nicholson *always* seems demonic to me. But for *Witches*, at least, that is exactly what is needed. Cher is striking and strong as Alex, and Michelle Pfeiffer did what she could with her limp role as suburban earth mother. Of the three female leads, it is Susan Sarandon who shines as the musician who transforms herself from mouse to bebop hussy overnight.

Go see *Witches of Eastwick*. Just don't expect too much. Prepare yourself for a mood swing mid-movie, and control your urge to throw your popcorn bucket at the screen in the final moments. And remember, any movie that totally subverts the misogynist bilge water of John Updike can't be all bad.

Steaming

Losey's Last Loser

Theater and film are not the same medium. This is a fairly obvious statement of fact. And yet many filmmakers have forgotten that simple fact over the years and have made some disappointing movies as a result. The major difference lies in the structure of the theatrical play. The physical limitations of the stage and Aristotle's theories on drama dictate that a play conform (give or take a little fudging) to the three unities of time, place, and action. All the action should happen in the same place over a short period of time.

Rules like that work fine in a theater, but they usually make for a dull film. Movies allow us almost unlimited visual and dramatic experience. That's what we like about them. The locale can jump from Nebraska to Venus to Malaysia over several centuries and *still* work. True, most movies don't wander that far afield, but they can. And even when a movie stays at home, we expect it to open things up, to expand our vision.

There is nothing worse than a static movie. (Okay, there are quite a few things that are *worse*, but few that are more tedious.) Regrettably, a static film is exactly what the late Joseph Losey made in his last movie, *Steaming*. Based on a play by Nell Dunn which was first produced in London and later saw a short run on Broadway, the film feels like it never left the theater, as if it were forcibly constrained by three walls and a proscenium arch.

Steaming takes place in a dilapidated, once-elegant Turkish bathhouse in London's East End. Women of all ages and classes take refuge there. Mrs. Meadows (Brenda

Bruce) and her daughter Dawn (Felicity Dean) are poor neighborhood women. Their home has a hole in the roof and no hot water. They come to the "Vapour Baths" to get warm and to clean their bodies. Josie (Patti Love), who is also poor, seeks shelter there when her lover batters her and leaves her. The bathhouse is the only place where she can relax and indulge in her sexual fantasies and dreams of a better life. Sarah (Sarah Miles) is a former jet-setter who has struggled hard to become a successful lawyer. She works nearby and comes to the baths to unwind and indulge herself. She invites an old school friend, Nancy (Vanessa Redgrave), to meet her there. For Nancy, a trip to the baths is a big outing. She is an upper-class displaced homemaker with grown children who remains tied to her empty house. Den mother to all her customers is Violet (Diana Dors), the manager of the baths, a practical but compassionate soul who offers what comfort she can in the form of a hot cuppa, a sympathetic ear, and a "good steam."

The action of *Steaming* takes place entirely within the confines of the baths, where the women sound off about their lives and the plight of women in general. The level of complaint is very much like the feminist (and quasi-feminist) dramas of the early 70s—anger and self-pity with little view to constructive action. Consciousness Raising 101.

Now, I'm as fond of bitching as the next woman (ask any of my friends), and a kvetch session can be entertaining. But *not* for two hours. And not when the bitching is so seldom insightful or humorous. The few scenes that are lively really stand out and let us know what could have been possible in a film like this. In one scene the women sit around and try to answer the semi-rhetorical question, "Why are men such shits?" In another, to my mind the film's finest moment, Josie confronts Sarah and Nancy with their classism. After she confides what she had to do to get her job as an exotic dancer (she was screwed by the proprietor of the club on a row of roller towels on the floor of his office), Sarah and Nancy show no sympathy. They claim that the

167

episode was her choice, and a poor one at that. Josie then follows them through the baths, letting lose a tirade against their condescension. "We're not friends," she yells. "I'm just part of the show you come to watch." She's right, of course. And the two women know it (but would never admit it). Instead they trade embarrassed looks, nervously jiggle their feet, and refuse to make eye contact with their accuser. It's a powerful scene. But one scene does not a movie make.

While certainly slim, the play's story line could support a movie. The women finally come together when the owners of the baths decide they are going to tear them down and build in their place a leisure club with an underground garage, a club few of the baths' current customers could afford to join. The women form an action group with the slogan "Save Our Baths ("SOB" their tee shirts proudly proclaim), and by the end of the film they win a tentative victory, with Josie as their spokeswoman.

The story and the characters are not what is wrong with this movie, nor is the acting at fault. The preformances are fine work. Vanessa Redgrave is particularly impressive as the sad and repressed Nancy. The problem lies with Joseph Losey's direction and Patricia Losey's screenplay, which manage to create an inert film.

The bathhouse is a wonderfuly designed set, and the camera work in it is fluid and intimate, but nothing seems to happen here. And for some strange reason the Loseys refuse to show us anything of the outside world. Why stick so rigidly to such a theatrical convention? Especially when other scenes would show how important the baths are to the lives of these characters. For example, why not show Josie in a confrontation with her battering lover, or the scene of her sexual harassment at the topless club? Why not show Nancy wandering around her large, well-appointed home, alone and lost? Why not show Mrs. Meadows, cold and sick, in her inadequate housing, or Sarah dealing with sexist garbage at the office? Or show any of these women's dreams and sexual fantasies, which are oft-expressed verbally.

There are countless scenes that would have further il-lumined these women's lives and expanded the vision of this movie, but the filmmakers used nary a one. We are not even allowed to witness the Council meeting where Josie carries the day by convincing the powers that be that the baths are an essential resource for the women in her community. Instead, the Loseys have the characters *tell* you about what they saw and what they did and what they felt. The audience is not allowed to see or feel any of it except in the most detached, indirect manner. Even actresses as talented as these have trouble conveying much emotional intensity given the turgid monologues and dialogues of *Steaming*.

There are so few films made about women, so few films that recognize that all women are oppressed. Even fewer recognize and express class differences between the oppressed or show women banding together to fight back in some way. And it is so seldom that film nudity is dealt with in a natural and unselfconscious way. (Heck, several of the extras actually look like real women, rounded bellies, thick thighs, and all!) *Steaming*, with its cast and its themes, has so much going for it that I would really like to recom-mend it. But alas, I cannot.

This is a film worth an evening of free small-screen view-ing when PBS puts it on the tube, but it is not worth paying five dollars to watch from an uncomfortable seat in a movie-house where you can't even get up and brew your own cuppa. It would be better to put the five dollars toward the steam, sauna, hot tub, or massage experience of your choice.

Aristotle has a lot to answer for in his restrictive view of the theater. But perhaps blaming the cinematic sins of Joseph Losey on the old fellow is going too far. The Loseys will have to take that rap on their own.

Of Lovers and Husbands

Heartburn

Nora's Revenge

Women have thought up many ways to avenge themselves on inconstant lovers through the centuries. But perhaps none has been as far-reaching, creative, *and* financially rewarding as writer Nora Ephron's vengeance upon her second husband, Carl Bernstein. They were both nationally known journalists, members in good standing of Washington's fashionable set, the perfect upper-yuppie couple before there was such a thing. Then, while pregnant with her second child, Ephron discovered that hubby was having an affair with the wife of Britain's ambassador to Washington. She took the kids, returned to New York, sharpened her pencil to a wicked point, and wrote a bitter, funny *roman à clef* about the whole thing. She told the world just what kind of faithless bum old Carl really was.

Now, many women would have considered themselves well-avenged at that point. Especially after the novel *Heartburn* became a best-seller. But Ephron wasn't content with exposing her ex to people who read books. She has gone a step better and aired her dirty designer sheets before the American moviegoing public in the new film *Heartburn*, for which she herself wrote the screenplay.

Rachel Samstat (Meryl Streep), a popular food writer, meets a fascinating new man at—heavy-handed irony here—a wedding. The audience knows all it needs to know just by paying attention to this scene, intercut with the opening credits. When Rachel asks her friends whether Mark Forman (Jack Nicholson) is single, they tell her he is "*very* single"—"famous for it," in fact. As the ceremony progresses, Rachel becomes dewy-eyed with emotion. Forman all but falls asleep.

Before you can say "irreconcilable differences," the two are in bed together watching a B-grade horror flick on TV and sharing a bowl of pasta carbonara Rachel has whipped up. Forman makes a sly comment about marriage, the kind of casual remark a man makes to assure a woman he doesn't consider her a one-night stand. But both are divorced and proclaim that they don't believe in marriage.

Proclamations are, of course, made to be ignored. And before you can say "mental cruelty," family and friends are gathered to witness the marriage vows of Rachel and Mark. But the bride, who takes the vows very seriously, develops a major case of cold feet. She has concluded that marriage doesn't work; divorce works. Family, therapist, friends all take turns coaxing her out of the bedroom, to no avail. And no wonder. Mark's best friends' version of encouragement is to tell Rachel that for twenty years Mark has been a cheat and a pig. "You're the only one he's ever treated decently!" they tell her. And, indeed, he *seems* to care when he makes the final successful bid to lure her from the single life. She concludes "I love you—I have to trust you," and the two are joined in wedlock.

All of the above takes place in the first ten minutes of the film. The rest of the movie consists, on a superficial level, of the rhythm of two successful, well-off people's lives as they build a life together and start a family. Of course, what it's really about is Rachel setting herself up for a fall and then, on cue, falling—a very pregnant Humpty Dumpty. But since Ephron and director Mike Nichols have made it obvious that Rachel is a stooge from the first moment of the film, there is little suspense to it all. And the film's few jokes and gags (most of which have to do with marital infidelity and the wicked ways of men) almost seem in bad taste with the awareness that they are at least partially at the expense of our heroine.

The heroine is the major problem with *Heartburn*. Not because of the performance of Streep, which is up to her usual level of excellence, but in the presentation of the character of Rachel by Ephron and Nichols. In the novel, Rachel tells the story, first person, past tense. It's all over. She is back in New York, older and wiser. Hindsight makes her bitter, but also very funny. She can marvel at her husband's treachery and her naiveté in ways that allow us to curse and laugh *with* her, not at her. In the movie, the character of Rachel is still central, but we have lost that sardonic self-awareness. Here we are shown a woman with "victim" written on her forehead who goes through the movie at first rather bemused in her happiness, then lost in a stupor of misery.

If I make it sound like *Heartburn* is a lousy way to spend a couple of hours, I don't mean to. There are some humorous moments and some touching ones—nothing to produce belly laughs or tears, but film bits that at least evoke a chuckle or a sigh. When Rachel leaves Mark for the first time and runs home to her father's empty apartment in New York, she veges out in front of the TV eating what we know, if we read the book, have to be butter-laden mashed potatoes out of a pan. After a stuffy pseudo-*Masterpiece Theatre* musical intro, John Wood appears with a devastating take-off on Alistair Cooke. He catches up the viewer on the latest civilized soap opera, and we are shocked to hear him detail the travail of our heroine, Rachel Samstat. It is an amusing piece of fantasy that shows us what the movie could have been like if the filmmakers had allowed us more of the voice and perceptions of Rachel.

Given its limitations, *Heartburn* can still be thoroughly

enjoyed as a performance film. Nichols obviously meant it as such, for the movie is filled with tight, almost static shots of his stars. We see mannerisms and facial expressions enough to keep any acting student fascinated. The scene wherein Rachel tells Mark she is pregnant with their first child is a perfect example of the intimate style of this film. Over a celebratory pizza, the couple think up and attempt to sing songs with the word "baby" in them. They hum, sing (garbling the lyrics badly), munch and masticate pizza, exchange glances, giggle, and otherwise act in a silly, mutually endearing manner. This scene culminates in a bravura performance by Nicholson of the "Soliloquy" (a.k.a. "My Boy Bill") from *Carousel*. (This is apparently an inside joke, since Nora's parents, Phoebe and Henry Ephron, wrote the screenplay for that famous film musical.) Jack sings the song badly but with much gusto and won't quit even when Streep's reaction changes from charmed to annoyed. It is the kind of slice-of-life theatricality that may have you glued to the screen. Or it may have you averting your eyes in embarrassment at a scene fully as intimate as the union of two naked bodies.

Since I think voyeurism is what film is all about, I really enjoyed *Heartburn*, despite the fact that the story line seemed to go nowhere. I wouldn't have wanted to miss Meryl Streep's performance for anything. She is the only actress I have ever seen who made me *believe* that she was really pregnant. This was not an actress with foam rubber strapped to her belly. This was a woman, seven months gone, who has learned that her second husband has taken his first lover.

Jack Nicholson's performance is a little less believable simply because it is a bad piece of casting. Nicholson is, after all, too old to play a bright, ambitious young columnist. He might be believable, with his crazed eyes and wild hair, as an axe murderer or a hitman, but a wunderkind of journalism? Don't make me laugh. Likewise, I might believe him as an aging philanderer who's too tired to go on, but as a young stud who's ready (or so he says) to settle down? Uh-uh. It's a good performance, but I didn't believe it for a minute.

The supporting performances are excellent. Stockard Channing and Richard Masur are a delight as Streep's and Nicholson's best couple-friends. I only wish that we learned more about them. The same could be said of Catherine O'Hara, of Second City Television fame. She is fun as a gossipy friend whose biggest joy in life is keeping abreast of who is sleeping with whom in Washington society. And an exquisite performance is given by two-year-old Natalie Stern as young Annie, Rachel and Mark's first-born. She smashes banana into Streep's face with total believability and a certain elan. And her bereft cries of "Mommy! Mommy!" when the harassed and heartbroken Streep leaves her behind are haunting. One would wonder how even a talented director like Nichols coaxed such a performance out of such a tiny tot were it not for the current rumor that Ms. Stern is none other than the real-life bairn of Ms. Streep. This kid is a natural for show biz.

I should also note the fine performance of Steven Hill as Rachel's benign but self-absorbed papa, a part central to the philosophy of the film. If Nichols and Ephron are making a point here, it seems to be that marriage doesn't work because men are polygamous jerks. When Harry Samstat finally returns to his apartment to find his pregnant daughter and grandchild taking refuge there, he has little comfort to lend. "You want monogamy? Marry a swan," he says as he hurries off to meet a lady friend. The filmmakers are certainly critical of men. Even Arthur (Masur), the most sympathetic man in the movie, has cheated on his wife. But, by implication, they are just as critical of women. "It is your own dumb fault to trust men, girls," they seem to say. And maybe they are right. But it doesn't make for a very cheerful movie.

At times, I felt about *Heartburn* the way I often feel about Woody Allen films (most notably the recent *Hannah and Her Sisters*). These are upper-class, self-centered cry-babies who can think of nothing better to do with their lives than to make one another miserable. The character I felt the most sympathy for was Della (Anna Maria Horsford), the housekeeper who gets stuck looking after Rachel and doing childcare for Annie when all she is supposed to do is clean Harry Samstat's apartment. I often want to give characters like Mark and Rachel a good kick in their Calvins and tell them to grow up. At least, in *Heartburn*, Rachel appears well on the way to doing just that as she takes a parting shot with her famous key lime pie, then packs up the babies and returns permanently to New York.

See *Heartburn* if you are a Streep fan (as who is not?) and if you enjoy American films that feel more like they're French. Or see it because it's one woman's incredible revenge. Think of Nora Ehpron getting rich as she rubs her husband's face in his infidelity. Revenge has seldom been so sweet.

Compromising Positions

Can This Marriage Be Saved?

In 1978, Susan Isaacs published her very successful first novel, *Compromising Positions*. It succeeded for many reasons, the author's smooth, witty style being one. But the real key to the success of the novel was its diversity. The book was equal parts homemaker rebellion, sexual farce, and murder mystery. In short, there was something for everyone.

Now Isaacs has translated her own novel into a screenplay, and the result has been translated into film by director Frank Perry with only moderate success. Perry, best known for angst-ridden films like *Diary of a Mad Housewife* and *The Swimmer*, is much too heavy-handed for sexual farce or suspense. He indulges us with a few chuckles and a couple of Hitchcockian touches (e.g., blood swirling down a dental spit-sink), but his heart isn't in it. He never seems at ease with wisecracking dialogue and sexual misbehavin'.

Judith Singer (Susan Sarandon) is a well-to-do homemaker from the prosperous Long Island community of Shorehaven. She has been married to her husband Bob (Edward Herrmann) for ten years and has two children, both now in school. She has never seriously contemplated how contented she is with her life, or felt compelled to get back to her career as a journalist (she is a former *Newsday* reporter)—that is, until a periodontist she once consulted is found murdered in his office.

Judith is contacted by the police both as an ex-patient of Dr. Bruce Fleckstein and because her Donna-Reed-perfect neighbor, Marilyn Tuccio (Mary Beth Hurt—in a wicked short hairdo), was Fleckstein's last patient before he was stabbed to death. The wholesome Mrs. Tuccio thereby becomes a prime suspect.

Also worried is another acquaintance of Judith's, a woman who confesses that she once had an affair with the lecherous Fleckstein, going so far as to allow him to take pornographic polaroids of her during their tryst. Mary Alice isn't the only woman to have transgressed with the randy rootman. When Judith attends the funeral, she comes to the slow realization that although the family is composed and dry-eyed in the front of the temple, every other woman in the place is crying her eyes out. Obviously the guy got around.

Judith investigates to protect the women she knows, but also to get her foot back in the door at *Newsday*. She has an inside source with the police via her lusty and profane best friend, Nancy (Judith Ivey). Nancy revives an affair with a young cop she calls Cupcake so she can pump him for facts while he does his own pumping.

It becomes clear that Fleckstein was a sleazoid who deserved to die. Not only did he seduce and abandon half the women in Shorehaven, but at the time of his murder he was under indictment as a child pornographer, too. So Judith starts digging, much to the anger of her husband. He wants a housewife, not a reporter, for a lifemate. When someone, probably the murderer, breaks into the Singer home and sprays MYOB (Mind Your Own Business) throughout the kitchen, husband Bob puts his foot down. The sacrilege of his hearth is too much. Judith will drop the case, or else.

Judith doesn't drop the case. Instead, she starts working closely with a sardonic homicide detective named Suarez (Raul Julia). At first Suarez views her as an interfering snoop. Later, he still views her as an interfering snoop, but he learns to appreciate her intelligence and her insights into the case. Soon he is wiring her to interview suspects for him and importuning her for a meaningful relationship.

Susan Sarandon does a good job with the role of Judith.

And I appreciated the fact that the filmmakers allowed her to look like a real woman. She does her chores and detecting wearing a minimum of makeup, grey sweats, and running shoes. She stays very casual and believable—we're given none of the ludicrous transformed-by-love/lust costuming and makeup so noticeable on Kathleen Turner in *Romancing the Stone*. Sarandon starts out playing Judith very tentatively, but gives her increasing confidence. Here is a woman who has lost the toughness of the journalist and has to learn it again.

Judith Ivey is *wonderful* as Nancy. She is salty, but never crass. Her wisecracks, delivered with just a touch of Texas drawl, are the saving grace of the movie. A homemaker who is also very much an uppity woman, she is a sculptor who enjoys frequent sexual relationships outside of marriage. And when I say enjoy, I mean enjoy. The fact that she is not humiliated and guilt-ridden at the end of the film is unusual and refreshing.

It is in the matter of men that Isaacs and Perry seem unclear and confused. (If it is any comfort to them, they are certainly not alone on *that* score.) Edward Herrmann plays the stereotypical yuppie workaholic, brainwashed as a boy into thinking his patriarchal family would run smoothly along the lines of "Father Knows Best." He plays the part of an egocentric jerk who gets increasingly shrill when things don't (i.e., his wife doesn't) go his way. Perry and Herrmann make Bob Singer such a disagreeable toad that his last-minute acceptance of his wife's journalistic ambitions seems unbelievable. It is hard to understand why Judith would want to stay with this guy.

Conversely, Raul Julia, as Lieutenant David Suarez, is a very attractive fellow, despite the fact that Julia sometimes appears to be sleepwalking through the role. Although he starts off officious and vaguely menacing, he is soon practically taking orders from Judith and loving it. At one point early in their relations, he mutters in exasperation, "You're not easy!" to which Judith replies, "Thank you."

The fact that he can accept, even appreciate, that she is not always the pliant female makes him seem very appealing as a romantic partner.

But in the movie (although *not* in the novel), Judith Singer resists the romantic temptation of Lt. Suarez. The last scene shows Judith working away at her typewriter, her friend Nancy stopping by to congratulate her on her front-page story and to chide her for not fooling around with her "major adorable" police suitor. Judith replies that Bob is a good father and tries to be a good husband, and looks back to her notes and typewriter.

As I walked from the movie theater, I confessed to the gentleman with me that I felt cheated. "In the book she goes for the affair. And why not? Nancy's right. The guy is major adorable!" To which my companion replied, "What's she going to do, marry the guy? He's no better. He's a workaholic, too. And probably treated his wife just as bad—which is why he's divorced. Singer makes really good money, at least."

Well, I was suitably mortified. He was right. The "happy ending" impulse dies hard, even in us long-time feminists. A romantic interlude with a cop is not what Judith Singer needs. What she needs is the freedom to pursue her writing career again. With the grudging acceptance of her husband, and his fat paycheck to support her and her children, she has that freedom. Free-lance journalism—an iffy income at best—might not be an option for a divorcée with two children.

So, which *is* the happy ending? That, my dears, is the million-dollar question. Was Susan Isaacs knuckling under to the demands of our current conservative climate by having her mid-80s movie heroine remain the virtuous wife? Or was she in fact providing us with a more realistic, even radical, "happy ending?" I don't know the answer to that one, either. I only know that I found this lightweight mystery movie surprisingly thought-provoking.

Jewel of the Nile

The Gem is Kathleen Turner

To see a woman face adventure with intelligence and physical bravery in a schlock film like *Jewel of the Nile* (or in the first—not to be confused with the second—Indiana Jones movie) may not seem like much until you realize how seldom it happens. Courage and smarts are still considered male characteristics in most popular culture. For example, I just came upon the following quote in a *1986* mystery novel by a fellow named Ross H. Spencer. His hero observes an active blind woman thusly: "This was a determined, highly intelligent woman who would get things done and to hell with the obstacles. She'd missed her calling in life. She should have been a man." Outrageous? Hell, yes. But even if Spencer realizes how comical and offensive that statement is, it seems unlikely that many of his male readers will blink an eye.

Fact is, we're still not considered capable of much. Noble self-sacrifice, unconditional love, yes. Gallant exploits, no. That is why I tend to be very forgiving with a film like *Jewel of the Nile*, which presents the exquisite Kathleen Turner as an adventure heroine named Joan Wilder.

Of course, Joan was not always an adventuress. In 1984's *Romancing the Stone*, Joan Wilder starts off as a world-famous romance writer who weeps at her own drivel and is too absent-minded to keep her Manhattan apartment stocked with paper products (after finding no tissues, toilet paper, or paper towels, she blows her weepy nose on one of the many shopping lists she has scattered around her apartment). Her editor, Gloria, played by Holland Taylor, who has

Kathleen Turner and Michael Douglas in Jewel of the Nile.

made a career out of playing funny, tough professional women, feels protective of Joan and is horrified when Wilder drops everything to fly to Colombia. Joan may be a shy woman who gets bus-sick, train-sick, and air-sick, but she sets off for the great unknown anyway when her sister sends a terrified SOS from South America.

I would like to say that in *Romancing the Stone* the character of Joan Wilder is transformed from a shy, homely, totally insecure woman by her love for her sister. But no. In standard romance novel and Hollywood fashion, Joan is transformed into a brave and resourceful woman with great beauty and perfect makeup (even in the dampest jungle) by her love of handsome man. The man is an extremely ego-centric but basically good-natured drifter named Jack Colton (Michael Douglas). Such a metamorphosis by love and a treasure hunt could have been thoroughly sick-making except for the lively, satiric script by Diane Thomas, some mercifully light-handed direction by Robert Zameckis (of *Back to the Future* fame), and an inspired performance by Kathleen Turner as the bodice-ripper author who sees her romantic fantasies come to life.

As entertaining as *Romancing the Stone* was, it did not cry out for a sequel. Few films do. But that never stopped Sylvester Stallone, so why should it stop Michael Douglas? Douglas, with his bland good looks, may be a miserable excuse for a swashbuckler as Jack Colton, but he is a savvy Hollywood producer. And having made megabucks off *Stone*, he eagerly pushed for the production of a sequel, almost over the dead body of his co-star. Turner didn't want to make *Jewel of the Nile*. It took both a stick and a carrot (a $25 million lawsuit and a reportedly gargantuan pay-check) to bring her back as Joan Wilder. And, Turner claims, equally important was her demand that the *Nile* script by Mark Rosenthal and Lawrence Konner be rewritten to give Joan more "spunk" and adventurousness.

The results are better than I feared, not as good as I hoped. *Jewel*'s story begins six months after the conclusion of *Stone*. Joan and Jack are now live-in lovers bumming around the Mediterranean on Jack's sailboat. He is playing and partying. She is trying to finish her new book, overdue at the publisher, and feeling vaguely dissatisfied. She's not sure what the problem is. Now that she's achieved the romantic solution, life still seems less than perfect.

Publisher and pal Gloria has no trouble seeing the trouble. She knows that Jack's sun-drenched hedonism and total lack of responsibility would get on any intelligent woman's nerves within six months. "His favorite author is the guy who wrote 'Pull Tab to Open'," Gloria scoffs, and advises Joan to dump him.

This she does, after a fashion. Or, rather, after a dashing leader from the north of Africa, Omar (Spiros Focas), convinces her that her next project should be accompanying him home to the desert to write his biography.

When Joan arrives in Africa she quickly becomes suspicious of her suave host. Omar claims that she is free to do and see anything she wishes. Yet her film is ripped from her camera after she snaps some graffiti reading, "Give Back the Jewel." And soon she is being kept under virtual house arrest in Omar's palace.

At this point our heroine, without any assistance from Mr. Colton, starts showing a little gumption. By spying in Omar's computer room she becomes convinced of his villainy. Then, as she skulks through the palace, she literally drops in on Omar's secret prisoner, a gentle Sufi holy man played with great sweetness by the juggler/clown Avner (The Eccentric) Eisenberg. It is this magician who is the "Jewel" of his people. Joan quickly vows to help the Jewel escape and reach the city where Omar has planned a spectacular proclamation of his rule.

Meanwhile, Jack has followed Joan to Africa, accompanied by his sad-sack nemesis, Ralph (Danny DeVito). The guys are less concerned about Joan than they are about capturing this giant jewel they keep hearing about. Still, Jack and Joan reluctantly join forces once more. Knowing that Jack is the kind of fellow who will "go around the world for a party but not across the street for a good cause," Joan fears telling Jack what (i.e., *who*) the Jewel really is. But the holy man advises Joan to believe that Jack is a changed man despite outward appearances, and he advises Jack to commit himself to his love. So much for the wisdom of holy men.

The trio take part in repeated episodes of action and slapstick. Enough to satisfy even the most jaded "A-Team" watcher. More than enough for me. We are presented with explosions, large-scale destruction, and general mayhem with no blood and little acknowledgment of the damage.

The name of the game is cheap visual thrills, devastation without guilt. Fleeing Omar's armed men, our pals jump into a jet fighter that none of them knows how to fly. But Jack throws off a quip about having played "Space Invaders," and they tear through a crowded marketplace without taking off, firing rockets and smashing their way through everything in their path while the natives scream and scramble for safety. All this rates nothing more than an apologetic shrug. Our heroes don't stick around to view the wreckage. For those of us who can't help but consider the consequences of actions, such a scene would be distressing even if it weren't taking place in a Third World country.

As for the Africa of *Jewel of the Nile*, it doesn't come off *too* badly. The locale is a strange hodge-podge. Omar seems to be a spoof on Libya's Muammar Qaddafi, while Nubians (one of the many groups our trio encounter) are long-time residents of the Sudan. The movie was filmed in Morocco.

Certainly it is easy to pick at the totally unrealistic portrayals of several African cultures, but the film's heart is more or less in the right place. Ralph may initially view the country as another "Third World toilet," but he is nonetheless transformed into something almost human by his experiences with a band of Sufi freedom fighters. He comes to love his Sufi brothers and even make peace with Jack and Joan following his trial by fire. What if he does view

Sufism more as a high school fraternity than a mystic sect? It's the thought that counts. All three of the Western characters are enriched (and not necessarily in a monetary fashion) through their visit to the Nile.

This is not to say that the producers don't snap at the chance for a little *National Geographic*-style titillation. When the Nubian women do their mating dance, Joan joyously joins in. The black extras who play the native women are all bare-breasted, but you can bet your Maidenform that Turner keeps her shirt *on*.

The director does not, rest assured, completely ignore his star as a sex object. We are treated to a lot of Turner's legs. Throughout her most strenuous exploits she wears a relatively short skirt, and you soon realize how much orchestration it must take to have a woman hang from buildings and climb mountains without a single glimpse of panty. They must have either reshot a lot of scenes or glued the skirt to her thighs! That's Hollywood. They couldn't miss any opportunity to tease moviegoers with Turner's gams, although even a cursory viewing of Kathleen synching background vocals in Billy Ocean's rock video of the movie's theme song, "When the Going Gets Tough," proves beyond a doubt that this woman is a vision in tux trousers, too.

How should one respond to a film like *Jewel of the Nile*? As nonjudgmentally as possible. It's nice to see women as strong and brave and attractive heroes in adventure films. Nonetheless, like Gloria, I fear Joan is wasting herself on Jack. But, as the standard mythology goes, the couple that hangs over a bottomless pit together stays together. Danger is the great unifier, proving true love. It doesn't matter that Jack Colton is a class-A deadbeat in everyday life. High adventure makes him seem very attractive.

Kathleen Turner's performance in *Jewel* is an undeniable treat. And for the rest of the film? It's a fairly amusing bit of escapist fluff—as long as you remember to hit the "off" button on your political consciousness when the theater starts to darken.

Peggy Sue Got Married

The Girl Can't Help It

Time-travel movies are nothing new. There have long been science fiction adventure films wherein scientists went backward or foward in time to study the way people live. But such films offer a rather detached view of humanity. Hollywood's most enduring and endearing time-travel movies take a much more personal approach to history. When Clarence the Angel allows Jimmy Stewart to go back in time in that sentimental Capra classic *It's a Wonderful Life* (one of my all-time favorite holiday movies), it is to see his own life. Or, rather, what life would have been like for his family, town, world had he never been born. *Back to the Future*, 1985's most lovable mega-hit, allowed teenaged Marty McFly to go back to his hometown in 1955, well before his birth, to meet and significantly interact with his parents as teens. Like these very popular films, *Peggy Sue Got Married* takes a personal approach to time travel. But, for once, the time-traveling hero is a woman.

Peggy Sue Bodell (Kathleen Turner) is an unhappy forty-three-year-old woman. She lives in a nice home and has two lovely children who are now young adults. She even has, we are told, a thriving business of her own (although we are never told anything about it). The major source of unhappiness in this lucky woman's life is her husband and childhood sweetheart, Charlie (Nicholas Gage), who has recently left her for a younger woman.

With the hurt and humiliation still fresh, the last thing Peggy Sue wants is a stroll down memory lane. But, wouldn't you know, the twenty-fifth reunion of the class of 1960 at

Buchanan High has arrived, and Peggy Sue, as majorette and all-round class queen, must attend. Her daughter (Helen Hunt) cajoles her into a silver bouffant prom dress and escorts her to the reunion dance, where she is miserable, forced to explain Charlie's absence to all and sundry beneath larger-than-life photos of her glorious lost youth.

It's enough to make a woman want to lie down and die. Peggy Sue comes close, collapsing when she is crowned reunion queen. When she awakens she is in the same gym, but the time is 1960. She has just given blood at the high school blood drive, and a youthful "Crazy Charlie" is stealing her Twinkie reward. Her two best friends (Catherine Hicks, Joan Allen) and the school nurse take her shock

Peggy Sue (Kathleen Turner) finds herself attracted to the class poet, Michael Fitzsimmons (Kevin O'Connor) in Peggy Sue Got Married.

and bewilderment for blood-loss wooziness and send her home—to her parent's home, where the long-lost past almost overwhelms her.

It's not easy to be a forty-ish woman from the 80s trapped in the body and life of a 1960 schoolgirl. Director Francis (whatever happened to the Ford?) Coppola and husband/wife screen writers Jerry Leichtling and Arlene Sarner certainly give us the comic aspects of the situation. Peggy Sue's modern sophistication and tendency toward psychobabble constantly puzzle her family and friends. When she first sees her prepubescent sister again, she is filled with love—and guilt for not having been nicer. Embracing the horrified girl scout, Peggy proclaims that "I want us to be closer!" because "I have too many unresolved relationships in my life." Her overtures are met, not surprisingly, with puzzled disdain from a kid sister who's never even heard of pop psychology and can only conclude that "teenagers are weird."

Much of the humor in *Peggy Sue* results from time-warp culture shock. Especially enjoyable is seeing the strength and directness of a "post-feminist" woman in an earlier society that expected more docility. It's great, for example, to hear Peggy Sue tell the class bully, "Get lost, you macho schmuck!" when he harasses the class nerd. It's even funnier to watch poor Charlie as he is constantly flabbergasted by his girlfriend's bold new attitude. When Peggy Sue suggests, while parking, that they "make love," he at first doesn't even know what she means, and, when he realizes that she means "sex...intercourse," his reaction is hilarious—part outrage, part fear.

The refreshing thing about the humor in *Peggy Sue* is that it is never overdone and never resorts to cheap gags or slapstick. Leichtling and Sarner take relatively few cheap shots at the innocence of 1960 America, and for that they should be commended. Even more than the humor of the situation, the filmmakers are able to convey the melancholy and loss of returning to one's youth. Every moment is a bittersweet revelation to Peggy Sue. When she sees her mother (Barbara Harris) again, it is as a contemporary, younger than she ever remembered her. In the movie's most haunting moment, Peggy is overcome when she hears the disembodied voice of a beloved grandmother (Maureen O'Sullivan), long-since dead, on the telephone.

Of course, the key relationships Peggy Sue re-explores are *not* those with girlfriends, grandmother, mother, sister, or even father. The focal relationships are those with Charlie and two other young men. With Richard (Barry Miller), the class nerd, she is able to share her secret—and futuristic clues for his brilliant inventor's mind. (Peggy encourages him to go "high-tech," but seems most eager that he make a killing inventing pantyhose.) With Michael, an intense young track star and beat poet in training, she is able to encourage his rebellion ("I'm gonna check outta this bourgeois motel, push away from the dinner table, and say, 'No more Jell-O for *me*, Ma!'") and live out a never-fulfilled sexual fantasy.

Charlie is her biggest problem and challenge. Knowing how he will betray her later, how can she stay with him? At the reunion she had offered the trite judgment, "If I had it all to do over, I'd do a lot of things differently." But when she again has to make the crucial decision of her life, the choice of mate and father for her children, changing destiny isn't so simple.

You see, Peggy Sue is still attracted to the adolescent Charlie, who, with his dirty blond pompadour and doltish charm, is "kinda cute." But it isn't her sexuality that betrays her so much as her compassion and emotional need. The grown Peggy Sue finds herself mourning the lost youth of her errant husband as intensely as her own. She is able to see clearly for the first time just how badly he wanted to be the next Fabian. She watches, with sorrow, as Charlie's dream of a musical career dies. Soon, she knows, he will give in to his father's blackmail and work full-time in the family appliance store. But, above all else, Peggy is genuinely touched by Charlie's boyish devotion to her. She had forgotten. Once upon a time, her husband really did love her.

Loving and wounded as he is, how can she reject him and change the course of her life? The answer is that she can't. And maybe that decision wouldn't gall the audience quite as much if Nicholas Gage weren't so miscast and misdirected as Charlie. Gage's Charlie often crosses over from awkward adolescent to twitching dumbbell. He brays, rolls his eyes, and jerks his neck and shoulders around like one possessed. He even burps in Peggy's face before kissing her. But why would Gage and Coppola *want* Charlie to be that unattractive unless they also want us to feel that Peggy is indeed wasting herself on a total geek who can't even be faithful to her in later life? Perhaps we are to view *Peggy Sue Got Married* as a tragedy and not just a heartwarming, if slightly melancholy, comedy.

Which brings me to my most troubling thoughts about the film. I have heard several people describe *Peggy Sue* as a female *Back to the Future*. It is not. *Back to the Future* is a cruder product, full of easy humor, action, and pyrotechnics. *Peggy Sue* is much more gentle and sophisticated, with as many tears as laughs. But that is only an external comparison. Consider the real message of the two films.

Back to the Future allows a teenage boy, Marty McFly, to go back and change life for the better. He is able to bring his parents together, improve the lives and lifestyle of his entire family, *and* save the life of his friend and mentor, Doc Brown. The movie is more than a well-crafted bit of light entertainment. It is an *empowering* vision of what a young man can do.

In a similar light, consider *Peggy Sue Got Married*. Here a grown woman (with much more wisdom and experience than young Marty) is totally unable to change even the course of her own life. The decision she makes isn't even an active one. She doesn't say, "My two children are so precious to me that I wouldn't want to miss the chance to be their mother." Or even, "It's worth it to stay with Charlie because it was so wonderful at the beginning." In her final scene in 1960, Peggy confronts her destiny, Charlie, in a storm-battered greenhouse and cries out that she "can't change anything" or "save anyone" (even herself). As fate decreed the first time around, she falls into his arms for their first sexual encounter—which, we know, will impregnate her and force her and Charlie to marry as soon as they finish high school. What a sad statement about a woman's powerlessness it all is—all the sadder because, I suspect, the filmmakers don't see it as tragic. Peggy Sue is not only powerless against the past but is also, apparently, powerless to control her future. At the movie's close there is every indication that she will take Charlie back as her husband.

Poor Peggy Sue doesn't even have the same comfort that Frank Capra gives his desperate hero in *It's a Wonderful Life*. Jimmy Stewart is at least shown what a miserable place the world would have been without him. He is validated—by an angel of God, no less—as a good person, essential to the well-being of hundreds, nay thousands, of people. The only comfort Peggy Sue is given is that of a possible reconciliation with Crazy Charlie, the Appliance King. Small comfort, that.

Perhaps it is unfair to compare *Peggy Sue* to any other movie. And it is, after all, a golden, sweet picture about coming to terms with the past, with lovely performances by Kathleen Turner and wonderful cast. Even if it falls apart a bit at the end, it is basically a well-crafted and entertaining film. But I cannot help but be distressed by the fact that, in a world of happy and successful male time-travelers, the female time-traveler is passive in and little enriched by her re-exploration of the past. Perhaps this is Coppola's attempt to bring existential reality to the time-warp comedy. If so, I can only say that I wish he had left it out of this particular movie. *Peggy Sue Got Married* presents the kind of reality we women have seen too much of already.

The Mysteries of the Modern Woman

Black Widow

Female-to-Female Film Noir

I grew up loving the old movies. At five o'clock every week-
day and often all day on Saturday and Sunday, I would glue
myself to the Philco and devour all those wonderful black-
and-white fantasies. One of my favorite movie formulas
(though I certainly had no name for it at the time) was film
noir: films like *Double Indemnity, The Maltese Falcon*, and
The Postman Always Rings Twice. The mystery angle was
fun, and (especially in the bad ol' days of the 60s) it was
refreshing to see a recognition (even in the good ol' days of
the 40s) of the corruption, desperation, violence, and yes,
SEX that are as much a part of the American soul as the
true love, happy nuclear families, and patriotic idealism
usually filmed. And then there were the women. Looking
back, I suspect that the key attraction those movies held
for me was their portrayal of powerful women.

Don't misunderstand me. When I say "powerful," I do
not mean *positive*. The women in film noir were temptress
sleaze bunnies, one and all. In their shoulder-padded, slinky
silk dresses, expensive perfume and cigarette smoke wafting
around them like an evil aura, they were the devil in a
decidedly female form. Like the devil, they tempted good (if

weak) men to do bad things at their bidding.

The killing of the "heroine's" husband is one of the most common of film noir crimes. But while Barbara Stanwyck, Lana Turner, et al. had the power to incite, they could not dispose of their husbands themselves. Except in their sexuality and their verbal duplicity, they were strangely passive. They had to depend on their young male stooge/lovers to actually do the deed. And, almost always, they were destroyed and survived by their impressionable young men, who, by rejecting the temptress, made some halting return to the path of light.

So where is the power in such portrayals? It's all relative. Noir-ish women only appear powerful in comparison to standard 40s screen images of women as faithful sweethearts and steadfast mothers and wives. Patriarchal culture

Justice Department special investigator Alex Barnes (Debra Winger, left) versus Catherine a.k.a. Marielle, Margaret, Rennie (Theresa Russell) in Black Widow.

relies on the old dichotomy of the mother and the whore. After scores and scores of movie "mothers," an unabashed "whore" was mighty refreshing. *That's* the power of noir women. These tough, beautiful broads had definite desires. They wanted sexual fulfillment. They wanted money and property. And like Tina Turner (and unlike most of their screen sisters), they wondered what love had to do with it. If only it weren't for that passivity!

Of course, the second wave of feminism challenged most of the cultural images of women. Since the late 70s, there have been more active heroines. The limited multiple choice of "mother" and "whore" has at least been supplemented by "both" and "none of the above." Film noir, which faded in the 50s and 60s, has recently experienced a revival of sorts (although some feel that film noir in living color is a contradiction in terms), with women's real-life empowerment altering the formula. A film like *Body Heat* (1981) appears to be in the classic noir mold. And it is, until you look at the portrayal of Kathleen Turner's femme fatale. She appears to suffer from the same old evil (and doomed) passivity. But appearances are deceiving. It is Lawrence Kasdan's brilliant play on this cinematic stereotype that makes *Body Heat* such a fresh variation on a familiar theme.

Now we have Bob Rafelson's film, *Black Widow.* In many ways this, too, is noir classique—but with some major changes, especially in the way women are portrayed. The key change is evident from the ads. "She Mates and She Kills" we are informed. Note the active verbs there. The femme fatale, brilliantly portrayed by the ravishing Theresa Russell, doesn't need any impressionable young buckaroo to do her dirty work for her. She kills her powerful publishing magnate hubby herself, and she has an airtight alibi: She was out of town. She returns, the grieving widow in black mink and dark shades, only long enough to destroy the evidence and cash in her chips.

The traditional noir-ish heroine would have quit there. Catherine doesn't. She changes her looks (to cheap flash and curls) and name (to Marielle) and marries herself another millionaire: a toy tycoon, Ben, played by Dennis Hopper. We know old Ben's days are numbered when Marielle visits her safe deposit box and extracts, from amid the pearls and cash, her secret supply of poison. For this femme fatale, once is not enough. As she will later admit with ironic candor, "I used to think of it as my job." After dispatching Hopper, she is off to further conquests: the career woman as deadly dame.

Although women in traditional film noir had a certain fatal fascination, they were never the central figure in those mystery melodramas. The real key figure was the male lover/stooge/avenger. In some cases, like Sam Spade in *The Maltese Falcon*, the seduced patsy and incorruptible nemesis are one. In other cases, like Neff (Fred MacMurray) and Keyes (Edward G. Robinson) in *Double Indemnity*, the roles are split. In all cases, the central character is male. Not so in *Black Widow*.

In *Black Widow*, one could certainly argue that the key figure is Catherine (a.k.a. Marielle, Margaret, Rennie), the murderous mate. But Rafelson and screenwriter Ronald Bass know that noir-ish suspense demands a relationship that incorporates sexual tension and the conflict of good and evil. So another central character is required. Instead of a Bogie, or a John Garfield, or a William Hurt, Rafelson has cast the role with another woman: Debra Winger as Justice Department special investigator Alex Barnes.

Alex (catch the androgynous name) is an ace 80s-style investigator. She spends little of her time on mean streets; rather, she constantly sifts through names and statistics at her computer terminal in a depressing government office building with wall-to-wall desks and painted-out windows. While tracking mob hits, Alex uncovers an unusual death: the apparently natural death of a New Jersey bigwig in his sleep of something called "Ondine's Curse." When more of these statistically improbable deaths of rich fellows occur, Alex looks for connections and eventually discovers one—the attractive, camera-shy widow.

This isn't the kind of case the Justice Department concerns itself with, and Alex's boss and assistant (Terry O'Quinn and D. W. Moffett) both encourage her to drop the case and return a little of their romantic interest in her. But Alex shows little interest in the wistful sexual yearnings of her co-workers. She *is* interested in and increasingly obsessed by the elusive woman who charms, marries, kills, collects, and moves on.

Early in the film, when Alex stands in her barren apartment studying the few slides she has been able to collect of her deadly widow, she superimposes her own hand and body over that of her prey, and then has a good cry in the bathroom. That episode is but a foreshadowing of Alex's own attraction to the woman she somehow identifies with, yet hopes to capture.

Catherine is such a creative and attractive figure (and her "victims" such shadowy and disgustingly wealthy male WASPs), it is hard for the audience not to cheer on this femme fatale's brilliant career. That is until, as Margaret, she marries and kills the shy millionaire anthropologist William Macauley (played with much sweetness and an excellent upper-crust American accent by Nicol Williamson). Macauley is a sympathetic figure. His death fuels Alex's guilt and resolve and forces the audience to side with the G-woman.

The scene then shifts to Hawaii, where our widow, now calling herself Rennie, has set her sights on a dashing French hotel baron. Alex tracks her down with the help of a wonderfully scuzzy private eye (James Hong). So begins a riveting approach-avoidance ballet between the two women. As we watch their I-know-that-you-know-that-I-know sparring, the divisions between the two blur, just as they did in Alex's slide show shadow play. Who is hunter and who is prey? Is the dynamic operating here love or hate? What are the motives of these two complex women? For Rennie, is it simple greed or bloodlust? For Alex, is it a quest for justice or a means of confronting her own fear (and possible hatred) of men?

Black Widow is an exercise in purposeful ambiguity, and nowhere is this more apparent than in the sexual lives of the lead characters. The sexual energy between Alex and Rennie is electric. The suspense of how it will manifest itself is just as powerful as that of the superficial mystery plot. When both become attracted to the same man (Rennie's current mark, played by Sami Frey), it is unclear whether their separate sexual liaisons with Paul are attempts to hurt or entrap one another, or whether this playboy pawn is merely the conduit of the lesbian lust they are unable or refuse to act out.

Mystery fanatic that I am, I am sorry in a way that *Black Widow* is a suspense film. I would love to discuss the finer points of plot and the significance of the film's ending, but that would be a dastardly thing to do to the few of you who have not seen this film. And for those few, my advice is to get off your duffs and go see *Black Widow* before it disappears from the second-run houses. This is an elegant thriller with stylish, subtle direction and writing, and superb performances by Russell and Winger. And if I can't discuss the ending, I can at least say that it shouldn't outrage or disappoint either feminists or mystery fans.

Let me also say that the relationship between these two women of mystery is the key to the whole movie. When Rennie says to Alex, "You know, of all the relationships I'll look back on in fifty years time, I'll always remember this one," we know she is being completely truthful. In my admittedly limited knowledge, I can think of no other film noir (and precious few movies of any type or description) where the relationship between *two female leads* is at the heart of the film. If only a movie like this had been available to Barbara Stanwyck and Lana Turner. Actually, there's still time. Are you listening, Hollywood?

Jagged Edge

Role Reversal in the Courtroom

I was *not* drawn to *Jagged Edge* because it was the one hit movie of the fall (1985) season. Box office boffo is usually reserved for mindless comedies about the cruelty and berserk gonads of youth—or, worse, for sweaty, macho fantasies in which the "good" guy commits murder an average of once every five minutes. *Jagged Edge*, despite two murders within the first five minutes, is nothing like the usual cinema winners. It is an old-fashioned murder thriller and courtroom drama in which the idealistic lawyer/hero is played by a woman.

The woman in question is Glenn Close, and she is the perfect choice for the role. Close, like Meryl Streep, projects fragility and vulnerability combined with iron-backbone strength, qualities that serve the part of Teddy Barnes quite well. Barnes is a veteran of San Francisco's district attorney's office, where she was a crackerjack young prosecutor until something soured her on criminal law. Nowadays she is the ornamental token woman practicing polite maneuvers in corporate law for a staid, old-money firm. That is, until she is asked to defend Jack Forrester.

Forrester (Jeff Bridges, way out of his depth in this one) is charged with the sadistic slayings of his wife and her Hispanic maid on a (what else?) stormy night in their luxurious-yet-isolated (of course) beach house. The murdered Page Forrester was an exceedingly wealthy heiress who owned an empire her husband ran for her. Stripped of his marriage, Jack Forrester would be nothing more than a hired hand, easily replaced; a divorce would have left

Jack with nothing. Motive enough for anyone, says DA Thomas Krasny (played with great intelligence by Peter Coyote).

As the police and Krasny try to build a case, one member of the prosecution team questions whether a man could take a hunting knife with a jagged edge and practically eviscerate his bound-up wife, but Krasny scoffs. Such an action, he says would be clever, not crazy; a husband would be more likely to get away with a crime that only a Manson-like madman could seemingly commit. Krasny assures his colleagues that he'd do it that way if he were going to kill *his* wife—clue number one that the DA is not one of the good guys.

Jack Forrester (Jeff Bridges), accused of murdering his wife, faces off with his defense attorney (Glenn Glose) in Jagged Edge.

In fact, Teddy Barnes was working for Krasny when she became so disillusioned with criminal justice, and we learn that much of the bad blood between Barnes and Krasny relates to the conviction of a young black man several years ago. When he conveniently commits suicide in prison at the same time Teddy's partners are trying to cajole her into taking the Forrester case, his death is the deciding factor in her agreeing to defend the rich widower.

And defend him she does. She prepares herself well, hiring a world-weary and profane retired investigator from the old days to help her prepare her defense. Robert Loggia is a joy as the crusty gumshoe with a heart of gold who loves Teddy and worries the case is a mistake; he believes Forrester guilty. But he plugs away, muttering non-stop expletives, and manages to uncover—with the help of an occasional anonymous note—some evidence that Forrester may not be guilty after all.

Meanwhile, Teddy's efficiency starts to deteriorate; she is obviously falling for her handsome client. Forrester passes his polygraph with flying colors, and she is told that he is either telling the truth or made of "the kind of ice that even the machine can't melt." The audience and Sam don't want to see her hurt, and, after all, it is hardly ethical conduct for an attorney to initiate a romance with his or her client in the middle of a case. Yet Teddy expresses little concern over her first kisses with Jack. And when things get even steamier after a racquetball game (ah, the sexual rituals of yuppies!), she murmurs only a few half-hearted "I can'ts," proving once again that women always mean yes when they say no.

Many viewers (feminists included) will wash their hands of Teddy at this point, and she does become a sap. When a surprise witness for the prosecution proves that Jack has lied to her, her hurt is more romantic that professional. She not only cries to herself but actually invades the home of the judge early one morning and weeps on his sofa, asking about hypothetical lawyers withdrawing from hypothetical cases.

Certainly director Richard Marquand and screenwriter Joe Eszterhas set Teddy up as a well-intentioned chump. But in all fairness, Teddy is *not* portrayed this way just because she is a woman. Anyone conversant with the plot lines of film noir and hard-boiled thrillers of the last forty years can cite many an instance of the honorable young man who thinks he's seen it all but whose naiveté and idealism are still touchingly apparent. He wants to do the right thing. He also wants to defend the beautiful woman who enlists his help and obviously has gotten a raw deal. Can she really be as innocent as she seems? Does she really love him? You know the story.

Jagged Edge is merely a case of role reversal, a modern film noir providing a woman equal opportunity to play the fool. Marquand is a little unclear on how to handle this reversal, however. It's almost as though he wants Close to play both the sap and the temptress. Why else would he have her pacing the courtroom wearing four-inch heels and a skirt so tight it is straining at the hips? Maybe this is the way staid corporate lawyers in the Bay Area dress, but somehow I doubt it.

One could also ask why Teddy has no female friends or associates in this film. Outside of her daughter (Teddy is briefly shown as the divorced mother of two), Close has essentially no contact with women off the witness stand. Her confidante is Sam, the father-figure detective. Male heroes in similar films are usually not isolated from their own kind in this way.

I doubt that either her femme-y courtroom attire or Teddy's lack of female companions was an unintentional manifestation of male chauvinism. By making Teddy appear increasingly feminine (the climax is precipitated by our heroine's housewifely instincts), vulnerable, and guilt-ridden about the American legal system, Marquand is setting the audience up for the film's climax. We must fear for her in the terrifying final minutes of the film. And we do.

Those who do not care for courtroom drama would do

well to avoid *Jagged Edge*. The film builds very slowly, and those who like constant terror or anxiety will find the lengthy legal wrangles far too dull. The ambiguities of this movie can also be frustrating. It is all well and good to toy with the concepts of good and evil and guilt, and the question of the guilt or innocence of Jack Forrester is supplemented by questions of the guilt or innocence of our legal system. It is the visual ambiguity, the murkiness of the cinematography, that is often maddening. We are shown anonymous notes we can't quite read (at least from the back of the house). And in the film's final seconds, when the murderer's identity is revealed, I have to admit that your eagle-eyed reviewer was unsure whose face she was seeing. (Outrageous as it may seem, the person next to me was equally puzzled.) It is the first time I ever had to ask the usher whodunnit.

Hey, maybe that's why this film is such a hit. People keep going back to see those final frames again, just to make sure.

The Big Easy

Love and Corruption in New Orleans

Ellen Barkin is one of my favorite screen actresses. Not that I've seen all that much of her. She has had a few small parts in semi-big movies (*Tender Mercies*, *Diner*) and a few semi-big parts in small movies (*Enormous Changes at the Last Minute*, *Desert Bloom*). But now, finally and at long last, she has a big part in a really big movie—the late summer (1987) hit, *The Big Easy*. On the ads and posters her name is listed below that of her co-star, Dennis Quaid (he is, after all, a man who's made a career out of playing outer- and *Innerspace* heroes), but at least it's *there* bold and brassy in nice sixty-point letters all over town.

Barkin's role in *The Big Easy* is a departure from the hard lives and open sensuality of much of her character work. The men behind the film recognized it as such a radical change that *Easy*'s producer, Stephen Friedman, is said to have originally threatened that Barkin would be cast only "over his dead body" because she was "too slutty." Luckily, director Jim McBride and co-star (and friend) Dennis Quaid were better judges of Barkin's abilities and the needs of the picture. Their fight paid off. Barkin brings great delicacy and conviction to a part that is essentially stock character and favorite 80s stereotype: the sexually repressed but professionally successful career woman.

Barkin plays Anne Osborne, a yuppie lawyer with the New Orleans District Attorney's special task force on police corruption. It is obvious from her no-nonsense manner of conduct and her ideas about right and wrong that she is an alien to life in New Orleans. (We're never told where she is from, but there is some indication that it's either New York or Boston. When asked, "Don't people dance where you come from?" she replies, "No, we barely spoke.") She meets the strange customs and attitudes of the natives head-on when she arrives at the office of Lt. Remy McSwain (Quaid), a half-Cajun, half-Irish cop who seems to be totally at ease with life in the Big Easy.

Remy takes everything—mafia hits, his love life—with a wide, almost goofy grin and a Gallic shrug. He'd rather trade wisecracks, casual endearments, and roughhouse antics with his co-workers than worry about the latest murder. A shotgunned corpse in a fountain prompts the casual query, "Who's the dead meat?" A stern, attractive D.A. prompts a more enthusiastic response in the form of open and persistent flirting. Remy enjoys a challenge.

And Anne *is* a challenge—sexually, but also morally. She is the troublemaker who destroys the police status quo of indifference and contented corruption, and the entire foundation of Remy's personal and professional life. It is not at all unusual for the female lead to be a troublemaker, the fatal woman, in a movie. But usually it is the force of her beauty and sex-charged femininity that does the damage. Here it is Anne's dedication to the law she represents and her ambition to get the job done.

If there is a sex-charged troublemaker in *The Big Easy*, it is definitely Remy, who is seductive in the most unself-conscious way. The movie takes pains to show that he is not a heartless cad, merely a man for whom artless cajolery is part of the enjoyment of the good life. He is seen with no other women. When not with Anne, he sleeps with his arms around a plush alligator toy. Yes, he is on the take, and callous about the murder of "wise guys," but in his heart, Remy is a moral innocent, the way Annie is sexual innocent. They learn from one another: he to grow up, and she to loosen up and enjoy life.

The problem with loosening something up is that force sometimes needs to be applied, which is fine if you're talk-

Remy McSwain (Dennis Quaid) is the easy-going New Orleans detective to Anne Osborne's (Ellen Barkin) up-tight assistant to D.A. in The Big Easy.

ing about a jelly jar lid, but not so fine if you're talking about a woman. No one is physically brutal to Anne, but Remy's courtship of her can best be characterized as psychological steamrolling.

It makes perfect sense, given Anne's unhappy history with men, and her valid concern about conflict of interest, that she should resist Remy's early romantic overtures. She repeatedly rebuffs him, but he refuses to take no for an answer. And so does the rest of New Orleans.

For example, when Remy drives up to Anne's office and tries to entice her into a date, using a pizza and a police report as bait, Anne at first turns him down. She capitulates only after the male driver penned in by Remy's creative parking cries out, "Go on, girlie, get in the car!" Anne's reluctance is repeatedly ignored by Remy and scoffed at by several other characters—most of them men. Her no's are again and again interpreted as shyness, embarrassment, and misplaced scruples, and are heard as yes's.

If you want to be enraged even further, let me tell you that this favorite male notion that a woman doesn't know her own mind is even applied to the film's "sex" scene.

This is the one scene all types of viewers have mentioned to me with considerable enthusiasm. And who can blame them? It is a very hot, very erotic screen interlude. You *could* get cranky about the fact that it is a sexually experienced man introducing a frustrated dress-for-success spinster into the joys of sex. You could really boil about the scenario of the seduction.

A confrontation over trust ripens into a heavy-duty petting session in which Anne is definitely a willing partner. But as the fondling escalates, she becomes embarrassed and withdraws from Remy, who continues his attention. She then asks him to "stop doing that." He doesn't stop, but rather challenges her to name what she wants him to stop. Arousal soon wins out over timidity, and Anne becomes an active participant in the proceedings once more.

Is your feminist outrage light flashing right now? If so,

it's certainly understandable from my written description of the scene. There is something about the power balance in this situation—experienced versus inexperienced, male versus female— that feels uncomfortable, possibly scary, and definitely politically incorrect. Feminist viewers have a right to be appalled. Some will view the entire movie as a nasty perpetration of the yes-means-no theory. And in many ways it is. But (dare I admit this?) while I was sometimes uncomfortable with Remy's wooing of Anne, I was never incensed by it.

I sat there and watched the screen and had to acknowledge that for this character in this situation, no meant if not yes, at least maybe. I *know* that this is a controversial image to put forward about women (or, indeed, anyone), but it is also, in some cases, a realistic one. A screen image can, of course, be both realistic *and* exploitive. I'll let you decide for yourself whether *The Big Easy* is exploitive. I only know that the *power* of Ellen Barkin's performance was such that I did *not* find it an exploitive portrayal of a woman.

My acceptance of the film's power politics comes not only from the way Barkin plays her role, but also the way Dennis Quaid plays his. Anne is conflicted, but not powerless, in this developing relationship. She is persuaded, but not conquered, by Remy. Barkin's gestures, her facial expressions, her intonation, all make it clear that Anne really wants this relationship, this lovemaking. And Quaid's Remy is not a dominant male figure. If you look closely at their courtship, you will see that Anne fully responds to Remy only after she has challenged him is some way, and he has in turn exposed his own vulnerability (or lack of power) through admission of insecurity, fear, guilt, or loss.

As for the "sex scene" itself, I found far more to commend than censure. I admire the way McBride and his two performers honestly conveyed all the complicated emotions possible between two people trying to make love for the first time. Embarrassment and fear are even stronger than lust.

211

The fondling is awkward and even painful—for *him*. When she apologizes that she is "not very good at this," our hero doesn't turn away or aggressively jump her bones. He is sweet and gentle and intent on pleasuring her.

While most movies would exploit such a scene as the perfect excuse for at least partial nudity by the woman (ignoring for titilation's sake the modesty an inexperienced and fearful woman would undoubtedly show at such a moment), *The Big Easy* goes for honesty over cheap thrills. Barkin plays the entire scene rumpled and partially un-buttoned, but fully clothed. It is Quaid who bares his buns—more than once—long before he bares his soul. (And a very attractive tushy it is, too!)

The Big Easy may be honest about the awkwardness of first lovemaking, but it remains steeped in romantic mythology to the detriment of its overall believability. First, you are asked to believe that man-about-town Remy, who originally hits on Anne because she *isn't* easy, and because he wants to know what she's up to in her investigation, quickly falls in love with her. As proof, the filmmakers pose that popular test of a man's serious intentions, that he holds his lover's head and wipes her mouth as she vomits into his commode, and then lets her use his toothbrush. Remy passes the test with flying colors, even before he gets all her clothes off.

You are then asked to believe that the love and trust established by Anne and Remy during their initial dalliance interruptus and in their later, off-screen consummation are so strong that they will not be destroyed when Remy is arrested the next day for extortion. Romantic that I am, I could almost believe Remy's sudden fall. I could *not* believe that an ethical hard-liner like Anne Osborne would, after what seems like only a token display of anger (which no one else takes seriously), stay lovers with a known felon.

More incredible yet, Anne is assigned the job of pros-ecuting Remy and doesn't withdraw from the case! Are we to believe that a principled D.A. like Anne doesn't know a conflict of interest when she sees one? Perhaps screenwriter Daniel Petrie, Jr. wanted to show that love has corrupted Anne in small ways, the same way love has redeemed Remy from his petty corruption. More likely, he thought opposing lovers in the courtroom would be a cute touch, a la *Adam's Rib*. Whatever his reasoning, he should have shown us Anne's motivation for such an incomprehensible action.

McBride and Petrie should have spent more time and care on quite a few aspects of the film. *The Big Easy* is one of the most entertaining Hollywood films I've seen recently, but it is far too ambitious for its own good. A love story that is also an action mystery and a serious study of the ambiguities of criminality is a tall order. Too tall. The end result is that the audience is likely to leave the theater feeling slightly cheated on all counts.

The Big Easy is, happily, weakest in those areas that matter the least—the action and suspense. You will likely lose track of all the players in this morass of drug deals and rival mafia clans. And McBride's big bang finish is rather clumsily orchestrated and exceedingly trite, reminiscent of "Miami Vice" at its worst.

As a study in corruption, *The Big Easy* has its moments. Remy, like his daddy before him, is basically a good cop, a good man, who is "on the take in little itty-bitty ways." But the line between petty corruption and hurtful evil is difficult to draw. When the woman you love says, "Why don't you face it: You're not one of the good guys anymore," it's time to mend your ways. Remy comes to see that what seemed a natural part of the job, a few harmless perks, is not necessarily harmless. He eventually sides with Anne against his brothers in blue.

Strip away the philosophical debates and the shoot-em-ups, and *The Big Easy* is primarily a love story. As such it is quite successful. Petrie's script is sketchy even in the romance department, but the chemistry between Ellen Barkin and Dennis Quaid makes up for any deficiencies in the dialogue department. Without words, these two are able to say volumes. Support performances are also strong, especially by the late-lamented Charles Ludlam as Remy's defense attorney.

While the action sequences of *The Big Easy* are no better than those of your average TV show, the relationship between the two romantic leads *is*. When I came home from seeing *The Big Easy*, I walked into the house and turned on the TV. (I admit it, I'm one of those people who *always* have the TV on!) Up càme the standard romantic confrontation from the standard action show. Barbie and Ken glared at one another from across the room and exchanged a few insults. Then Barbie, lips quivering, admitted that she missed the big hunk. The two passionately kissed, noses and heads tilts perfectly aligned. Not a hair, an item of clothing, a smidgen of make-up out of place. Two seconds later, he was on top of her.

How I wished I were back with Ellen and Dennis. She with her squinty eyes and bumpy nose. He with his floppy hair and doofus smile. They look like real people. Best of all, they act like real people: clumsy and fallible and needy. And loving.

Fatal Attraction and
Someone to Watch Over Me

Sex and the Single Terrorist

The current obsession with the "new" monogamy would be hilarious if it weren't so depressing—and so based in gut-wrenching fear. The fear of AIDS is the most obvious source of the current sexual paranoia. But it's not the only reason our popular culture is once again embracing the simple, cracked logic that love and marriage go together like a horse and carriage. When Carly Simon (former troubadour of the exciting, cynical world of sexual freedom in the 70s) admonishes her girlfriend to stay in her dull long-term relationship because it's "The Stuff That Dreams Are Made Of," she isn't playing on her (or our) fear of AIDS. Her message is rather that a good, or at least bearable, man is exceedingly hard to find. Once you latch onto one, you'd better stick like a leech.

This warning against the single lifestyle and toward a "Stand By Your Man" monogamy reflects the agonized frenzy the media has tried to stir in the hearts of single female baby boomers during the last few years. Our biological clocks are at two minutes to midnight, they keep telling us. And, as *Newsweek* gleefully warned in their infamous article of June 1986, women in their thirties have probably already missed the boats when it comes to finding a husband. Once you hit forty, it's all over. In their immortal words: "Forty-years-olds are more likely to be killed by a terrorist" than to marry. The message is: You tarried too long with your freedom, girls, and now you've got to pay. You're used goods. No one would want you for a life partner. You used to scoff at the nuclear family. Now you realize that you'd kill to have a hubby and bambinos in your own golden little house.

Of course, when *Newsweek* preaches a sermon on the desperate plight of single women, can Hollywood be far behind? Enter two tales of the horrors of spinsterhood masquerading as thrillers, *Fatal Attraction* and *Someone to Watch Over Me*.

Fatal Attraction is one of the cleverest examples of woman-hating to ever roll off a movie reel. Adrian Lyne, creator of such slick trash as *Flashdance* and *9 1/2 Weeks*, has done it again with a movie which continues to gross a million dollars *a day* weeks after its release. The premise of the movie is a simple extension of *Newsweek*'s statistics. When the alarm on a woman's biological clock goes off, she becomes a demon that will not be denied. If she's more likely to be killed by a terrorist than find a husband, she's likely to *become* a terrorist to get what every woman is in heat for—a "suitable" father for her children.

Alex Forrest (Glenn Close) is just such a terrorist. And the nastiest thing about Lyne's portrayal of this woman is that she doesn't start off looking or acting like a terrorist. When we first see Alex, she is at a crowded cocktail party to launch a new book on Samurai self-help. She is a particularly cool, beautiful, and completely self-assured blonde in a room full of sleek and attractive New York yuppies. When she cuts dead the rather crude flirtation of a not-very-sleek schlump, we may (as Lyne hopes we will) think her a bit of a ball-breaker, but her reaction seems reasonable enough. Later, she is perfectly gracious (and mildly flirtatious) with the schlump's colleague, Dan Gallagher (Michael Douglas). And when Alex and Dan meet again at a legal huddle where she, as editor, is called in to discuss a suit against one of her author's books with Gallagher, the publishing house's attorney, she is calm, intelligent, and professional. She is also clearly interested in Dan.

As Lyne carefully builds the attraction between his two

leads, it is hard to mistake the power balance. Although Dan is portrayed as the handsome and bright rising star of his law firm, in social-sexual matters he is seen as a klutz and an innocent. Here is a guy who gets cream cheese on his nose eating a bagel, who can't open his cheap umbrella in the middle of a downpour, and can't seem to catch the attention of cabdrivers or waiters. He is bedazzled by Alex's come-hither looks and her cool sophistication. When the two discuss, playfully, whether or not to end their friendly dinner in bed, Dan acknowledges that the choice is hers. Decision-making power belongs to Alex because she is the stronger personality of the two and Dan doesn't know his own mind. Of course, according to the filmmakers, any sexual situation where the woman is empowered is a situation ripe for disaster—a feminist violation of the natural order.

When the decision is made, by Alex, to defile this married man, Lyne and Close (in a brilliant, haunting performance) start to build their image of imbalance and iniquity. Alex brings Dan back to her stark white loft in the middle of the meat-packing industry: a she-devil leading her prey past smudge pot fires and hanging animal carcasses to her own little hell. She makes love to him in a pointed debasement of domesticity, among the dirty pots and pans in her kitchen sink.

While the sex, expressed in all the exaggerated panting and moaning of cheap porn, is good for Dan, it (and Alex) are clearly too much for this simple, domestic fellow. When Dan tries to toddle home, Alex turns petulant and possessive and eventually self-destructive. Dan is puzzled and dismayed. How could a simple roll in the hay suddenly get so complicated? It is a philandering husband's worst nightmare when Alex refuses to play by "the rules" that say that a woman who sleeps with a married man has no rights, no power. Such women do not deserve loyalty, tender consideration, or respect in the morning, say those rules. The fact that Alex does want, indeed *demands*, these things is proof of her insanity, which becomes more and more pronounced from this point on.

Meanwhile, Dan's lovely and sweet wife, Beth (Anne Archer), knows nothing of her husband's betrayal. She tends to their adorable daughter Ellen (Ellen Hamilton Latzen), and plots to buy an even cozier nest for her family in the country. Dan confesses his infidelity only after little Ellen's bunny rabbit is found dead and boiled in the Gallagher kitchen. The sides are then drawn in this life-and-death struggle for suitable husband material; the good/chaste/suburban/wife/homemaker must fend off the attack of the evil/sexy/urban/slut/career woman. When the Mother and the Whore do battle, can the victor be in question?

To reinforce the message that single women are the enemy of married women, and that married women must reject, if necessary destroy, their unnatural and envious sisters, Lyne makes use of another popular anti-feminist stereotype: that of the emasculated modern American man. Dan is seen as a passive victim, a tethered goat to Alex's predatory female. At home he is un-macho, too. His approach to his wife is less sexual (i.e., dominant) than worshipful. And unlike his own father, he is nurturing and approving toward his daughter. Sounds good, except that Lyne's point seems to be that tenderness makes a man a total wimp. When Dan has both the opportunity and provocation, on two separate occasions, to protect his family by killing Alex, he is unable (despite the loud encouragement of the movie audience) to be effectively violent. Destruction of the temptress is therefore left to the enraged lioness protecting her den and cub. Beth doesn't hesitate: She blows away her rival with a single shot to the heart.

The fact that such a story is doing such boffo box office is due in part to Lyne's clever direction, James Dearden's tight scripting, and excellent performances by all the lead players. But this is by no means the best movie of the year, nor does it boast any superstars in its cast. *Fatal Attraction* is a mega-hit for other, more disturbing, reasons. It feeds into the general public's deepest fears about single, successful (read: feminist) career women and the danger they represent to the nuclear family. When Alex challenges Dan's professed happiness in marriage with "So what are you doing here?" or when she later informs him, "I won't let you treat me like some slut you can bang a couple of times and then throw away like a piece of garbage," she is being strong and assertive and justly angry at "the rules" of a male-dominated society. Yet by making Alex a self-destructive madwoman, Dearden and Lyne are encouraging us to equate a woman's independence and anger with madness. They are also trying to convince us that the single woman's confidence and success are merely a mask for her deep-seated self-hatred at her failure as a real woman. She is a monster without the Day-Glo eyes or the bloody fangs or other accoutrements of the fantastical fiend. Alex is no fantasy. Lyne and Dearden want us to believe that she is real.

And the unmarried, career woman monster is one Americans, even women, need little encouragement to believe in and hate. At the show I attended, a young woman sitting in front of me joined the throng in egging Dan on to murder and in clapping and cheering when Beth finally shot Alex. This woman, as the filmmakers hoped, identified strongly with Beth. As the shot rang out, she yelled out, "Take that, Bitch. I'm sick of your shit!"

Someone to Watch Over Me would probably evoke a less dramatic reaction from my young friend. It is a very similar film, made with just as much visual style by Ridley Scott. But *Someone* doesn't ask us to hate the single woman, only to pity her. Claire Gregory (Mimi Rogers) is the single woman in question, a wealthy member of New York's beautiful people. At a fashionable club, Claire is the only witness to the murder of a friend by a mafia-connected psychotic named Venza (Andreas Katsulas). While she has a rich, anal-retentive lover (played to perfection by John Rubenstein), he's another of those emasculated American males. He doesn't even make a pretense of protecting her. He leaves town soon after the murderer threatens to kill Claire.

Now, even if her boyfriend were no help, a rich woman would still have plenty of resources to call on for protection. This is a woman who could easily afford to hire an army of Sly Stallones (or Brigitte Nielsens) to protect her day and night. But what kind of story would that make? Claire is instead portrayed as a frightened, isolated (evidently she has no family or real friends) woman who must rely on the kindness of strangers: namely the New York Police. One of her guardians is a good-looking, happily married joe who just made detective. Mike Keegan (Tom Berenger) is your basic, boring, lower-middle-class cop. Like Dan Gallagher, Mike Keegan is a bit of a klutz. Unlike him, he is still a man's man capable of protecting a woman.

Police detective Mike Keegan (Tom Berenger) finds himself torn between his wife (Lorraine Bracco, right) and an elegant East Side murder witness (Mimi Rogers) in Someone to Watch Over Me.

In fact, when Mike strays from monogamy, it is not because of the lure of Claire's she-devil sexuality, but because Claire shows herself to be a weak, womanly woman. She collapses, weeping out of her terror, and Mike offers her sex as a pledge of his comfort and protection. Unlike the monstrous Alex, Claire admits that she has no claim on Keegan. She is pathetically grateful for any attention or help she can get from a manly, good-looking husband type like Mike.

Meanwhile, Keegan also has a nice wife at home, an ex-cop named Ellie (Lorraine Bracco) who is not appeased when he tries to soften the blow of his infidelity by sobbing out, "I respect you so much!" Ellie knows how much such proclamations are worth, and she doesn't try to soften the blow at all when she decks her husband in a restaurant parking lot, screaming "Don't talk to *me* about *respect!*"

Let me say here and now that the little spirit and warmth found in *Someone* all belong to Lorraine Bracco in her first major screen role. Bracco is able to perfectly blend a genuine toughness and strength with all the expected attributes of the idealized Hollywood homemaker. Ellie, unlike Beth in *Fatal Attraction*, is allowed her sexuality and her full measure of anger toward her husband. When Keegan is expelled from his cozy home, Ellie becomes the household protector. In a short, hilarious scene, she takes her son to the practice range to watch as she polishes her shooting skills. She is still quite a markswoman, but instead of aiming for the heart, Ellie shoots out the groin area on her paper target with much grim satisfaction.

The dynamics of the triangle in *Someone* are much different from those in *Fatal Attraction*, since the real enemy is the male murderer and not the female interloper. Claire is never a villainess, just a lonely woman in need of help. Neither woman sees the other as the enemy. In fact, Claire freely offers to put herself at risk when the bad guy threatens Keegan's family. But, as in *Fatal At-*

traction, it is the lioness who saves the day, blowing away the villain to protect her son and husband.

Even without the rigid Mother-Whore roles, there is no question who will win and who will lose in this movie. After the shooting is over, the Keegan family unites in (I kid you not) a group fetal hug. The nuclear family is re-solidified, and poor Claire is left out in the cold, in the dark.

And *that* is what both of these films are really about. The most poignant, pointed, and exploitive scene in *Fatal Attraction* is not, to my mind, the murder of Alex and her unborn child by Beth. It is a much earlier scene when Alex stalks Dan home to his new suburban home. It is winter, and Alex is shivering in the dark and cold. She peers into the window of the Gallagher living room like a child at a toy store. Inside, Beth and Ellen snuggle in the golden glow of their fireplace. Dad comes home after a rough day to this peace and joy. The three form an enchanting tableau of the perfect beatific family unit. Alex stumbles away from the window and vomits.

While *Fatal Attraction* expresses a much more virulent form of misogyny than *Someone to Watch Over Me*, both of these flashy thrillers argue that the nuclear unit of mommy-and-daddy-and-baby-makes-three must not be put asunder. And since the heterosexual nuclear family unit is *the* natural order, single women are the ultimate losers in life. *Fatal Attraction* tells us to hate the unmarried woman as an unnatural and evil creature. *Someone to Watch Over Me* tells us to pity her for her sterile and exposed life. Both tell us that an unmarried woman deserves what she gets—as long as it's bad.

As I thought about these movies, another pop song came to mind, Maggie Roche's "Married Men," in which she lists her various conquests among the attached male population. The song ends: "All o' that time in Hell to spend, for kissin' the married men." The Roches are being ironic when they make that statement, but the same cannot be said for the boys in Hollywood. Adrian Lyne, and many of the thousands of people flocking to see *Fatal Attraction*, really see the single woman as a social evil deserving of fire and brimstone.

Scary? Definitely. But, call me an optimist, maybe the unmarried uppity women of the world should be cheered by the woman-hating of these films. After all, the single woman's blissful independence must be viewed as a serious threat to the patriarchy to warrant such open attacks in the popular culture.